# Praise for
# *Falling in Love with a Buddha*

Frank Berliner's spiritual memoir is beautifully crafted and written. It is a tale about love, and the great longing that springs from there—to learn, to grow, to be real, and to forge a genuine connection with oneself and others, with life, and with death. I highly recommend it.

—John Welwood, author of
*Toward a Psychology of Awakening*

With sensibilities at once romantic and coolly analytic, Frank Berliner trains his considerable powers of observation, recollection, and composition on three principal topics: his spiritual father Trungpa Rinpoche, his biological father, and himself. The book swells with wry humor, sex, death, and other compulsively readable stories of a real spiritual encounter. It is a profoundly moving volume on what will be the shelf full of books recalling Chögyam Trungpa Rinpoche. This one also looks, without embarrassment, at the work that men must do to love.

—Acharya David Schneider, author of *Street Zen*

Frank has written an exquisite and heartfelt memoir, full of the experience of *dharma* woven together with the Western literary stream—the ivy league meets crazy wisdom—and Frank eloquently teaches throughout, creating a work that is a transmission in itself.

It is also the quintessential and lively portrayal of Buddhism coming to America, seen through the eyes of a young man falling in love with a Buddha and taking him to "meet the parents," literally and figuratively, with always unpredictable and surprising results.

The pages radiate with what Chögyam Trungpa described as the experience of "nowness"—living fully in and for the present moment but thoroughly appreciative of one's own lineage and heritage. In that way it is a gift for the "lonely" American practitioner on a path of devotion and self-awareness.

—John W. Cobb, president of Naropa University and author of *Footnotes to the Inexplicable*

# FALLING IN LOVE WITH A BUDDHA

## *A Spiritual Recollection*

For Liz,

In the sacred Dharma.

Frank W. Berliner

5·13·2012

# Falling in Love with a Buddha

## *A Spiritual Recollection*

Frank W. Berliner

ALL MY RELATIONS, LLC
Boulder, CO

On the cover: Chögyam Trungpa Rinpoche's teaching chair, with the TigerLionGarudaDragon emblem of Shambhala.

ALL MY RELATIONS, LLC
Boulder, CO


Published by All My Relations, LLC



First Edition
Printed in the United States of America

Cover design by Alex Musat
Book design by Gail M. Nelson

ISBN 978-0-9851790-0-7

10 9 8 7 6 5 4 3 2 1

# Dedication

For my mother, Esther Ann, and my wife, Nan.

# Thank You

With special thanks to Gregg Campbell, whose
encouragement and generosity
made the writing of this book possible.

*Who will remember you when I have gone,*

*My darling ones, or who remember me?*

*Only in our wild hearts the dead live on.*

—May Sarton, "Death and the Turtle"

# Contents

# Author's Note

This book has come into existence as the result of my meeting an authentic spiritual master when I was twenty-eight years old, and resolving from then on to dedicate my life to studying with him and serving him.

This memoir is inspired by the simple reality that I was fortunate enough to be alive when he was alive; that in every interaction with him, he seemed in some utterly uncanny way to embody the raw truth at the very heart of life; and that, at very rare and always unexpected times, I seemed to have been paying attention when he did.

My teacher was a wild holy man. He changed my life and the lives of many, many others in ways that we are only just beginning to fathom. In that sense, this book presents the story of my life as only one reflection in the radiant mirror of his life. It is certainly not the story of his life in any complete way, since none of us who knew him could ever write about more than the few reflections each of us saw in entering his world. Like the blind men touching the elephant in the Buddha's parable, each of us encountered only one facet of his enormous life, and we each interpreted that encounter according to the particular limitations of our own consciousness.

This is also a book about a father and son. It recounts my history with my own father, whose impact on my life was powerful and profound, both painful and inspiring.

Finally, it is about how my encounters with my teacher clarified and healed my relationship with my father, even if that was never his real agenda or intention. Indeed, beyond communicating the urgency for each of us to wake up fully in our own lives, I have no idea what his real agenda or intention was. In that sense he was, and will always remain, unfathomable.

Now both are gone from this world, and the finality of death compels me to say farewell to them both, as all sons must inevitably say to their fathers. Yet the blessings of each are more and more vividly present in my own life as I grow older. For this, my gratitude to each of them is endless, and "Farewell!" becomes "Hello again!" every day—even every moment.

# Prologue

"How late?"

My father is at the wheel, as always. We are driving to Boston so that he and my mother can hear my Tibetan Buddhist teacher, Chögyam Trungpa, for the first time. I have just given them fair warning that Rinpoche, as his students call him (it's a traditional honorific for high lamas, literally "precious one"), is often late, even for his public talks.

Nearly sixty years old, my father drives as fast as he did when I was a boy, but his reflexes are no longer quite what they were. Though he still loves being at the wheel, I no longer love being in the car with him when he drives.

When I was a boy, I found the experience quite wonderful. As a young pediatrician in the 1950s, he made house calls to tend to the sick children and worried mothers of the town where I grew up, less than twenty miles from New York City. At times he would allow me to go with him. I would sit happily in the car while he went inside these houses, his scuffed leather doctor's bag in his right hand. I was old enough that my pride in traveling with him outweighed my jealousy that he was devoting so much of his time and energy to other people's children.

Being in the car with him was always a great adventure, especially on longer outings when we would visit his older brother's family in far-off Washington, DC each spring. The cherry trees all over the capital were in bloom and their vibrant pink clouds of blossom ornamented those pristine white marble memorials to all the venerable, long-dead fathers of our country. Daffodils bloomed in every garden. We hunted for colorful Easter eggs that our aunt had hidden in their backyard. I fell in love with my pretty cousin at first sight and at age seven experienced for the first time the pain of unrequited affection.

Returning home from those family pilgrimages on Sunday afternoons, as we approached New York City along the crowded main route through New Jersey, my father would bypass the long, stalled lines of traffic by driving brazenly along the wide-open shoulder of the highway for miles at a time.

"Oh Ben, don't do this!" my mother would plead, almost in tears from her anxiety and embarrassment. "You're setting such a terrible example for your sons!"

"Do you want to get home today or tomorrow?" he would reply. He asked with such sincerity and conviction that you couldn't help but believe he was posing a choice to her that was actually real.

"Why can't you be like everyone else on this road?" begged my mother. "Look at these hundreds of cars. None of them are doing what you're doing."

"Don't worry about it, honey. They just don't have any imagination," he said. "I've got my MD plates, sweetie pie, and the police aren't going to give us any problems." His tone, at once both arrogant and reassuring, foreclosed any further communication. As always, he had the last word.

He leaned toward her and patted her cheek with infuriating charm and tenderness. Then, with his arm resting on the sill of his open window, he continued cruising along that narrow asphalt corridor without a care in the world.

From the backseat, my little brothers and I cheered him on. It was thrilling! The steady breeze through my father's window caressed our faces and spurred us to bold new heights. Riding shotgun, as it were, we imagined we were performing a vital service to my father by keeping a close eye out for cops. My mother turned away, gazing out her closed side window with a look of utter resignation …

Nearly twenty-five years later, we're in the car together once more. My father at the wheel, my mother in the front passenger seat, and I in the backseat, but without my brothers now on this spring evening in New England.

"I can't tell you how late. I can't even tell you for sure he will be late. But he often is, so I thought I should just give you a heads-up."

"Why is he late?"

"Maybe it gives people a chance to practice patience, Dad. I don't know."

"It sounds pretty rude to me."

My father seems now to drive even faster. One might think he would slow down at the likely prospect of Rinpoche's being late so that he won't have to sit in the lecture hall quite so long to wait for his arrival. But on the contrary, it's as if being on time is, for him, a matter of such supreme, personal honor that he wants to witness every moment of Rinpoche's dishonorable lateness firsthand.

"Ben, please don't drive so fast," my mother pleads. My father slows down ever so slightly, then gradually inches back up to his previous speed.

"At the hospital, I give medical students five minutes," he proclaims portentously. "I give residents ten minutes and associate professors fifteen." He is now chief of pediatrics at an urban medical center. The days of humble house calls in the old neighborhood are long past. Their four children have all left the nest, and my parents have relocated from asphalt Long Island to leafy Connecticut.

"Then what?" I ask.

"I leave."

"Oh, I see. The higher the rank, the more slack you cut them?"

"You've got it."

I try to imagine where Rinpoche falls in this hierarchy, but don't pursue the matter any further. My father puts a well-worn recording of Beethoven's *Fifth Symphony* into the tape deck of the car, turns up the volume, and continues speeding toward his rendezvous with my teacher in Boston.

Ninety minutes later we sit in the lecture hall with several hundred others, waiting.

Rinpoche is already half an hour late. My father looks at his watch incessantly and taps his feet impatiently. All around us people are talking to each other quite cheerfully. Obviously, many have been alerted to Rinpoche's *modus operandi* and are adapting themselves to it without resentment. No solemn spiritual hush here! The hall is bubbling over with animated conversation.

"When you really think about it," says a woman directly behind us, "Tibetan Buddhism is the mystical wing of American Judaism." My father overhears her and glances back over his shoulder. His natural curiosity gets the better of his irritation for a pivotal moment. What a fascinating thing this young lady has just uttered! And that she is quite attractive only compounds the interest as far as he is concerned. For the first moment since spotting a red-tailed hawk in a tree by the highway in Rhode Island two hours ago, he forgets all about the time.

"Excuse me," he says, using his sweetest tone and most charming smile. He turns around fully to explore the matter further with her. "What exactly did you mean by that?" Immediately they are engaged in an intense and wide-ranging conversation about the younger generation of American Jews. About how their disillusionment with their parents' superficial and materialistic approach to their ancestral roots has led them, first to radical political activism, and then, disillusioned with that, to a spiritual practice that isn't based on believing in God.

My father, a Jewish doctor and trained evolutionary biologist who has never believed in God and who especially dislikes what he regards as the smug, childish certainties of organized religion of any kind, is intrigued.

"Are you a student of Rinpoche?" he asks her at last.

"Yes, I am."

"And what does he believe in?"

"He doesn't seem to believe in anything, as far as I can tell."

"That doesn't sound like spirituality. It sounds nihilistic."

"Not at all."

"Why not?" He is riveted by her confidence and directness.

"Seeing things as they are isn't based on belief."

"What the hell does that mean, 'Seeing things as they are'?"

"It means not having any preconceived ideas about what you're experiencing," she replies. She is not even remotely intimidated by his blustery challenge—the one he habitually uses to disarm any potential adversary.

"But do you really think such a thing is possible?"

"Of course."

"How?"

"Meditate."

Abruptly she stops talking to my father and looks beyond him, up to the stage. As if on cosmic cue, Rinpoche has materialized from behind a curtain. He is sitting in a big chair on the stage and smiling as broadly as the Cheshire cat. The audience quickly quiets down. The long-awaited talk begins …

As we drive back to Connecticut an hour later, I ask my father whether he feels that Rinpoche was worth waiting for.

"Yes," he responds.

"In what way?"

"I liked his sense of humor."

"When?"

"Often. Especially when he said that enlightenment has to have 'light' in it—but light as opposed to heavy, not as opposed to dark, like the usual religious stuff. That was good." He considers for a moment, then adds, "I'm not used to a talk on religion having a sense of humor. It was refreshing."

"But Buddhism is not a religion, remember? It's spirituality."

"You know what I mean. Don't be a wise guy."

"Was there anything else?"

"What is he drinking up there? It's not clear enough for water. White wine?"

"Sake, probably."

"Why?"

"I guess he likes it." I've heard this question often enough that I no longer attempt a more complex explanation than this.

"It seems strange for a Buddhist teacher to be drinking alcohol while he teaches."

"I agree that it's unusual."

My father pursues this no further. We drive in silence for a while.

"Anything else about your impressions of Rinpoche or his talk?"

"Yes. The way he answers people's questions," says my father with his characteristic decisiveness. "He answers them, not just their question. He answers them behind their question," he continues. I marvel, once again, at my father's unique blend of skepticism and genuine appreciation.

"As if he knows what you're thinking even better than you do," adds my mother. "It's uncanny. It gave me chills."

"Did he persuade you to meditate, Dad?"

"I wouldn't go that far," he says with a chuckle and shoves the *Fifth Symphony* back into the tape deck once again.

"I think I'd like to try it," says my mother, just ahead of the wall of sound that now engulfs the car. This time Beethoven has the last word. We spend the rest of the drive in a familiar mode—a captive audience to my father's undying enthusiasm for those majestic, pounding chords.

Years later, I'm told that when Rinpoche was asked what he thought of Western classical music, he replied, "Beethoven made aggression respectable."

# PART ONE: LOST HORIZONS

# Chapter 1

I come ashore as a single droplet within the tidal wave of births in the United States that has since come to be called the baby boom. It is six months after Hitler has taken poison, two months after the United States has dropped the first atomic bomb on Hiroshima, and five days after the United Nations charter is ratified.

The war is over, America has won, and millions of young, horny soldiers and their eager wives are immediately getting down to the important business of reproducing themselves as often as possible. The pulsing lifeforce of a crude, blind optimism is everywhere. Lines of identical, mass-produced houses march over the helpless potato fields of Long Island, and the rural idyll of my father's boyhood is bulldozed under in the process.

My father was not a soldier. His childhood asthma disqualified him. On a healthier note, he is already a doctor—a young pediatrician whose work was considered in some way vital to the American cause. Though he was not at the front, he found a dignified form of alternative service in his medical role. The medical profession confers its privileges. And being a pacifist at heart, he was probably quite relieved not to have to go overseas and kill people.

My uncle, his younger brother, is a pilot in the Far East. Though the war there ended in August, he remains in Asia for several months afterward. On the day of my birth, he sends my father a telegram from somewhere across the Pacific congratulating him on his first son's arrival. I am told later that when he returns, he comes to live with my parents in their first house and shares a room with me for a few months.

I always feel a strong bond with my uncle as a boy. Like my father, he is expressive and emotional. Even more than my father, he likes to give hugs, and he cries easily. I always feel that he saw things in the war that made him permanently sad, and that also made him feel life is precious and family very dear.

As a boy I am affected by a photograph of my uncle in his military uniform, in my parents' family album. This image of him is woven into other childhood experiences in my own idiosyncratic way. My parents love to listen to Puccini operas, especially *Madama Butterfly*. When the naval officer Pinkerton sings, I picture him as my Uncle Bill in his uniform. A few years later, when I see the young Marlon Brando in the film *Sayonara*, I feel he looks a lot like my uncle.

My mother, too, had a brother who was a pilot in the war, but I never met him. He was shot down over China in 1944, flying a dangerous mission for the American military support of the Chinese Nationalists under Chiang Kai-shek. There is a photograph of him in that same family album as well. He is tall, lean, and strikingly handsome, with upright posture, a square jaw, and sparkling eyes. His open smile is frozen in perpetuity there in black and white at age twenty-two; he could easily be mistaken for a young Gary Cooper.

Even now, my mother can never talk about Uncle Charles without anger and sorrow. She feels he was a mere pawn in a cynical and brutal chess game of political power, and that he was cut down before he ever had a chance to live. And of course, she is right.

Indeed, my mother herself was piloting planes before she met my father. I still have a photograph of her standing next to her little Piper Cub, ready to climb up into the cockpit. She is twenty years old. Her hair is luxuriant and windblown and she looks happy and glamorous. She is a beautiful young woman. My father says she looked like the actress Gene Tierney then. She learned to fly so that she could go to rural areas of the country to provide medical care for poor people.

*My mother in front of her Piper Cub, circa 1941. Photographer unknown.*

My mother is so idealistic and naïve when my father enters her life. When they meet, she is a nurse-in-training, and he a resident in medical school. He charms her on their first encounter, shamelessly praising the beauty of her bright blue eyes. From that moment on, he grounds her. She gives up her airborne dreams, they marry, and together they build his pediatric practice back in the town where he grew up. They start their family, beginning with me.

My father is the son of a Jewish meat dealer, and my mother the daughter of a Methodist minister. Her mother, with no attempt to conceal her anti-Semitic sentiments, warns her daughter not to marry him. She gives two reasons: "His people talk with their hands" and "He will never put you first." The day of their marriage, both remember vividly, is more like a wake than a wedding.

As far as not being put first is concerned, it seems that I too am a casualty of that prophecy. Though I have no memory of the actual event, since I am only six weeks old.

Shortly after I'm born, I'm told, I develop a hernia on the left side of my abdomen and have to return to the hospital in New York for surgery. It's a weekend, and somehow my father persuades my mother that it would be fine to just drop me off there, while he and she take a much-needed little vacation at Montauk Point, on the eastern end of Long Island. After all, they are working very hard to get his practice up and running. They will retrieve me on Sunday evening. And so it comes to pass.

I do not get the full story of this event until I'm a forty-six-year-old graduate student in psychology, doing a research paper for a child development class. At that time, I ask my parents to send me their own individual accounts of the incident without consulting the other.

My mother writes that she has never forgiven herself for not staying with me in the hospital that weekend. She remembers that her husband's attitude had been strongly influenced by Dr. Benjamin Spock, who encouraged millions of postwar parents to wean their children early in what can only be described in retrospect, at best, as benign neglect.

My father writes that it was a routine surgery and that he's quite sure it had no negative effect on my psychological development.

In an interesting coincidence, the same year that I research this medical version of an original sin in my parents' relationship with me, I develop a painful hernia on the right side of my abdomen and must have it surgically repaired.

Though my mind cannot recall being left alone as an infant under the surgeon's knife, apparently my body has not forgotten.

It is summer. I am four years old. I sit on the front porch of my parents' home, watching the traffic pass by, hour after hour. I am enthralled by the trucks, which appear only seldom, but always with a grand rumbling and roar to herald their arrival.

I only have eyes for them. I marvel at their grilles, which look like great teeth; at the bulging, blazing eyes of their headlights; at their immense size and overwhelming sound; at the uncountable number of wheels they have, though I try to count them; and especially at the giant revolving abdomen of the cement mixer and the dribbles of wet cement it defecates freely and arrogantly on the pavement as it passes.

"I drive that truck!" I proclaim with great pride whenever an especially impressive specimen rolls by …

At night my brothers and I stand on our beds in the big room we share like three little characters in a Grimm's fairy tale. The lights from passing cars shine through the window and slide along the walls of the room, illuminating each of our bodies in turn in the darkness. The game is simply to strike the wall in front of you just as the shifting light hits it.

We keep score; we argue in fierce whispers over each other's claims of success. We are absorbed, thrilled by the competition. No one ever wins. The game ends when an unintended shout of excitement brings our father to the door. He stands in silhouette, the light from the hallway behind him.

"That's enough, boys. Time to go to sleep." His voice is gruff, but not really. We subside.

After he leaves, I lie there on my bed, feeling the coolness of the night on my skin, watching the lights from the road move gently and silently around the walls 'til I fall asleep …

Then there are the great mountains in a wonderful picture book in the bookcase of my parents' living room. Page after page they rise, impossibly steep and high, encased in white snow and turquoise ice, with deep, cloudless sky all around and above them.

"That one there is Mount Everest, the highest mountain in the world," says my father omnisciently, pointing to a picture of a soaring black pyramid framed forbiddingly in pristine, blue-black space.

From that day forward, I draw Everest and all the lesser peaks in its royal domain again and again on vast dioramas of butcher paper that my dear, patient mother keeps providing for me. I work tirelessly in the big back bedroom, happy and alone and free from my brothers.

I'm obsessed with which of my majestic peaks will finally be Everest. I continually revise the outcome with the lordly whim of the Creator, drawing each peak slightly behind and slightly higher than the last, hour after hour.

Then at long last, it's that one—there's Mt. Everest! I call my mother in to confirm the reality of my creation. I am happy …

I study pictures of tigers in another book. I am in love with their fierceness and power and beauty, their glowing yellow eyes that compel such fear and admiration. I imagine befriending one, then being eaten by it. Told that there are real ones in the zoo, I cannot rest until I see them in the flesh. But there, they turn out to be so disappointing, listless, and sad. The smell of their cages makes me want to retch. I run from the House of Big Cats as fast as I can—but not, alas, out of fear.

Not until many years later, when I read William Blake in college, do tigers arise again in me, "burning bright, in the forests of the night," and not 'til then do I realize that it is the tigers of the imagination, not the real ones, that abide forever, fierce and vivid and invincible …

And the babies of the town in their seemingly endless procession of carriages, wheeled by their doting mothers back to the office behind our house. There, my father and mother, omnipotent doctor and attentive nurse, seem to receive them all with equal cordiality. The old Judy Garland song my father sometimes sings to my mother takes on a painful new meaning for me:

The birds are singin' for me and my gal
And sometime, I'm goin' to build a little home
For two, or three, or four, or more,
In Love-land, for me and my gal.

It's three at first—my father, my mother, and me—and that's fine. Then four, then more, as my two brothers come along in less than three years. And now more, then more, as I watch the parade of other people's children past the front yard fence, day after day. My fantasies, full of jealous rage, are all variations on the same theme. Remembering the soft spots both of my baby brothers had on the tops of their heads, I imagine pounding my little carpenter's hammer through the crown of every little interloper who perambulates past the front yard fence …

One day, my father reveals to me the shocking truth of Santa Claus's nonexistence. He asks me to keep the secret from my younger brothers for now, but I tell them, and then ask them not to tell him I told them.

Of course they do.

How disappointed in me he is! He shakes his head, telling me without words that I cannot be trusted with a secret.

My father walks next to me in the backyard one spring. Perhaps he has coaxed me down from my secret perch in the big pine tree near the pond, the place where I go when I want to be alone. The cherry tree and forsythia bushes are in full bloom, as are the clumps of iris, daffodils, and tulips that my parents have lovingly planted. Even now, when I close my eyes and remember this garden after the passage of more than fifty years, I experience a vivid, sweet mingling of happy and sad together.

Fifteen years later, in a college class, I come upon lines from Andrew Marvell's poem "The Garden" that would have given voice to this feeling then had I known and understood them, and give voice to it still:

> Meanwhile the mind, from pleasure less,
> Withdraws into its happiness ...
> Annihilating all that's made,
> To a green thought in a green shade.

Yes, even at the tender age of eight my heart is distilled to its very essence in my parents' garden—distilled to a green thought in a green shade. I am overflowing with blissfulness and wonder, and to be free of my younger brothers, to be alone with my father is such a rare thing by this time. Our backyard seems an entire vast cosmos, brimming with an ineffable presence that is radiant and benevolent. There is something invisible but real beyond what is visible, like purple aureoles radiating above each purple iris.

*My father in his greenhouse, circa 1950. Photograph by Doris Ackerman.*

"David's dad says there's a God. Do you think there is?" I ask him.

"No, I don't think there's anyone or anything in particular behind all this," he says. "I think it all just is."

"But who started it?"

"One thing just led to another, and here we are."

"So we're alone?"

"No, we have each other. And we have this beauty." He smiles down at me.

He says it all with such matter-of-factness and confidence—the way he says everything—that I know he must be right.

He loves poetry and reads it or recites it aloud whenever the inspiration of the moment strikes him. His favorite is "Fern Hill," a poem by Dylan Thomas. Recalling my childhood days in the springtime in my parents' backyard, I think of its lyrical opening lines: "Now as I was young and easy under the apple boughs / About the lilting house, and happy as the grass was green …"

It is comforting, and even magical, after my father's death, to discover that there is a recording of him reading that poem, probably from around this same time, when he was in his mid-thirties and still overflowing with a theatrical, romantic vitality. His voice on the tape exults forever: "Time let me hail and climb / Golden in the heydays of his eyes."

And also to discover a photograph of him from this time, perched up in the branches of the majestic cherry tree in full bloom. His face is dark and handsome and his hair still very black, but cut short in the military style men wore then. (Alas, it was a style that he continued to impose on my brothers and me until each of us at last went off to college and escaped his implacable command.) He is looking out wistfully but content through the pink cloud of blossom, a cigarette between the fingers of his dangling left hand. It's the early 1950s in postwar America, and everything in his relaxed, lordly posture proclaims that life is good, indeed.

But I myself am not always so easy, being young. One afternoon, I am feeling especially bereft at my parents' absence. I picture them surrounded by the usual adoring crowd of mothers and children in the sanctum behind our house that I am never permitted to enter while they are working there. I grow more and more disconsolate, then angry.

At that moment I come upon a crippled robin beneath my favorite pine tree, at the foot of the yard. I remember vividly the funky smell of the muddy duck pond a few yards away and the warm, fading afternoon light filtering through the needles of the pine.

The robin's small, dark eyes look at me calmly, but as I step near him, his trembling body makes only the slightest, halting movement. He has been hurt. He cannot fly away. Without a moment's deliberation, I pick up a rock and crush him.

I bury the broken little body quickly and furtively. The next day, gnawed continually by shame and remorse, I confess to my father. Though not at all pleased, he is not unkind. It is very confusing to confess to him. I feel my own headlong fall from grace, yet feel at the same time that he is somehow the cause of it, though I have no words to express to either him or my mother why this is so.

More deeply still, I realize that it is not my parents' approval or grace I feel cut off from now, but something immeasurably deeper, a very different kind of loneliness. Other than swatting flies and slapping mosquitoes, I will never kill another living creature.

I learn, too, that there are places in me as dark as the bright ones are brilliant.

# Chapter 2

On my twelfth birthday, my father gives me his copy of *Lost Horizon* to read. As he hands it to me, he tells me that it is one of his favorite books. When I ask him why, he replies that it is a story about a world that human beings long for most in their heart of hearts, even those who don't know it yet.

"What kind of world is that?"

"A world where people don't have to kill each other."

"Like your best friends, Al and Ben, who died in the war?"

"Yes, like them."

"But it wasn't their fault that they were killed, was it?"

"No. Not at all."

"What was that world called?"

"Shangri-la."

"Where was it?"

"They say it was high in the snow mountains of Asia, near Mount Everest somewhere."

"What was it like? Very cold?"

"Not according to the stories. It was in a hidden valley that didn't get snow, but had lots of flowering trees."

"Like our garden?"

"Perhaps."

"What else?"

"It was beautiful. It was a place that protected all the best books and paintings and music that people have created, all hidden away from the killing and violence of the rest of the world, so they wouldn't be lost and destroyed. The people there were gentle and kind and very wise."

"Did Shangri-la ever really exist?"

"You should read the story yourself, and make up your own mind about that."

Reading it, I reflect further not only on how my father lost his friends in the war, but on how he himself never served because of his asthma. Like Conway in the book, he escaped the violence and madness that engulfed so many others. Is this why the book spoke to him so particularly? In losing his dearest friends, was it as if he too had served? Or did he feel the guilt of the survivor? I never asked him. But he always abhorred war and never glorified it in any way.

Years later, when he is eighty-three years old and pitiably frail with the lung disease that will end his life in less than a year's time, we go to see *Saving Private Ryan*. It is the first time I can remember that he and I have ever gone to a film without anyone else.

As the horrific violence of the landing on Omaha Beach grinds on and on in the opening scene, his body begins to shake and he weeps uncontrollably. I lean over and hold him like a child. It will be the only time he ever lets me do that.

He seems to weigh barely more than a bird.

It is my first year of high school. I am fourteen years old, playing in a school tennis match. It is a brilliant, windy autumn afternoon; violent gusts make it difficult to keep the ball in play.

Suddenly, a tall boy from the opposing team falls on the neighboring court. Before I even notice that he has fallen, he is dead.

As we wait for the ambulance to arrive, I look at his body lying there on the asphalt. His face has turned blue. His lips are puffed out. The suddenness of it is incomprehensible, terrifying. Someone brings a blanket to cover him. His teammates are weeping. A few minutes before, he was chasing a tennis ball; now he is dead and will never be alive again.

There is no place yet in my sheltered world to truly absorb this stark realization. Because I never knew him, or his name, and was not playing with him when he fell, I tell myself this is not really happening. But the wind, as if to mock my efforts, gusts wildly and blows the blanket covering the corpse up against the chainlink fence. There he is again, blue and swollen, daring me to deny it.

The match is cancelled. I ride my bike home, looking back at the familiar tennis courts with strange new emotions.

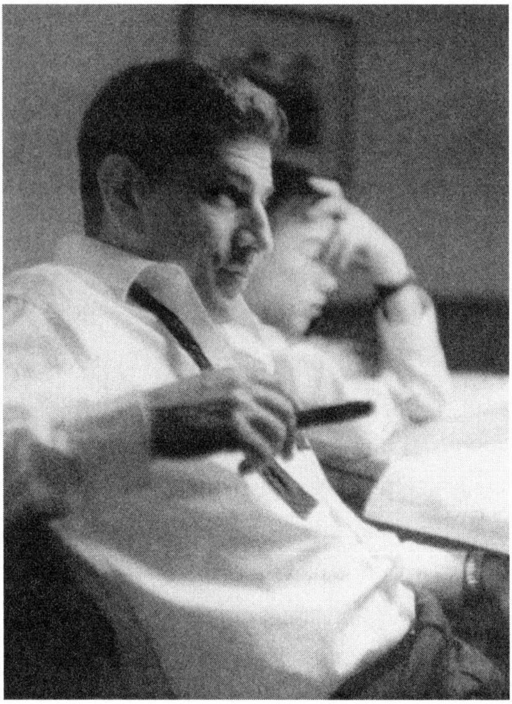

*My father watching the telecast of JFK's election returns on November 8, 1960, with me in the background dozing off over homework.*

# Chapter 3

Only seventeen years old the day I attend my first class there, I'm a freshman at Yale. Beyond having pleased my father by choosing it over Harvard, and after the initial heady excitement of finding myself in such a prestigious world begins to fade, I really have no idea why I'm here.

I have even less of an idea what I want to do with my life afterward, or how to make use of the privilege of being here to gain even greater levels of privilege later on—something that, to my amazement, many of my classmates already seem to know exactly how to do.

As my college years fly by, this feeling of confusion never really leaves me, despite the many accomplishments others applaud me for. No victory seems to point to any future possibility that I can visualize with the slightest enthusiasm. There's a gnawing, underlying sense that I haven't a clue who I am or what it has to do with this venerable, intimidating place.

Late in October of my freshman year, I am awakened in the middle of the night by the ringing of a telephone, followed soon after by the piteous sound of one of my roommates weeping. He is a shy, gangly boy from a public high school in Amarillo, TX. Studious and pious, he has seemed from the beginning utterly out of place among all the smooth, blond preppies who stroll the campus in chuckling cliques under the bright golden elms and maples.

The sound of his grief in the dark touches and frightens me, but I pretend to be asleep, not knowing what to say or how to reach out to him. Next morning I learn that his father has died unexpectedly. His face is still red and raw with crying as the cab driver stows his suitcase and he leaves for Texas. "My dad was a minister," he says quietly.

He returns to Yale a few weeks later to pack up his belongings. I never see him again.

Then, only three weeks later, another brilliant, windy autumn afternoon arrives. It's the most important weekend of the year—the Friday before the Harvard football game. The whole campus is humming with anticipation. Hundreds of cocky young men wait for their girlfriends to arrive by the busload, the local hotel is booked solid, and the drugstores have already sold out of condoms. Classmates stand out on the commons, throwing footballs and "snagging bennies"—catching the beneficial rays of the sun—on this unseasonably sunny day late in November.

My high school sweetheart isn't coming, as time and distance have already begun the inevitable erosion of our passionate adolescent bond. But I haven't had the time, or the heart, to replace her yet. I'll be attending The Game alone, if I attend it at all.

I go to my Friday-morning art history class, definitely my favorite. There, I am equally entertained as educated by the dramatic photographs the celebrated professor took of the Parthenon and by his spellbinding lecture, which elucidates its mysteries. When he finishes, he gets a standing ovation. Ah, to be a teacher like that—he is probably the first rock star I've ever seen! I walk back to my dorm, inspecting Yale's architecture with a new, more appreciative eye, and dream idly of being a celebrated professor myself someday. I will teach my students about the great poets and write my own poems on the side …

An hour later, I try to escape my approaching loneliness by retreating to my room, pulling down the shades, and going to sleep.

"Wake up! Kennedy's been shot!"

I awake abruptly to find my remaining roommate's face looming over me, his eyes wide with astonishment. Having delivered this surreal message, he turns and rushes back to the room across the hall. That's where the only TV in the dorm is—enviable property of an elite confederacy of four wealthy roommates. They hail, incredibly, from Georgia, Alabama, Mississippi, and Tennessee. Even before I enter their dominion I can hear them laughing and celebrating. One of them has already broken out the bourbon and the rum.

On the screen in the background I can see a grayish talking head and hear Walter Cronkite's familiar voice—grave and slow and disbelieving. Then, uncharacteristically, the voice cracks just a little. The whole thing is now irreversibly and undeniably real. JFK is dead.

"Oh Jack, oh no, no, they've killed my husband, Jack, Jack!"

The laughter and hooting reach their peak. Glasses clink; someone offers me a drink. I turn around and flee the room abruptly without saying good-bye. Twenty minutes later I'm on my way to the New Haven train station, heading home to spend the weekend in the familiar and comforting embrace of my family, where I can weep without shame along with everyone else. Later, I learn that when the Harvard game was postponed until the following weekend, some of my classmates were outraged at the inconvenience and the extra expense.

Kennedy's murder reverberates within me throughout my four years at Yale. For at least a year I can think of little else. I have the heightened sense of having woken up to the stark reality of being a stranger in a strange land. I feel achingly how little I have in common with the vast majority of my classmates.

It's also a shock to see how naïve I have been in my smugness about the political and cultural certitudes I've inherited from my family. I realize, with some measure of shame, that I am still a child. I see plainly that there are hundreds of sharp, confident, forceful young men all around me who share little or no agreement with me about what I believe to be true. I see that what I've been nourished on since childhood is not immutable truth, but merely one opinion about how things are. It is a long, hard fall.

I feel that the rifle shot in Dallas has opened a gaping hole in the now hopelessly idyllic universe of my boyhood. And it is pried open again, day after day, by the recurrent—and astonishing—thought that a man of Kennedy's grace, wit, confidence, decency, and power can be slaughtered in broad daylight for the entire nation to witness.

And even more horrifying is that whoever did this unspeakable thing walks away from it unpunished. I feel an almost paralyzing fear that if this can happen to such a person as President John Fitzgerald Kennedy, then there is no real safety, not to mention justice, anywhere in the world.

*How could they do this? How could they get away with it?*

Truly the universe, as the existentialists I'm studying in one of my lit classes proclaim, is absurd and devoid of any abiding meaning. Sartre is right: "Man is a useless passion." Such are the thoughts of a romantic young man in a philosophical black hole, whose worldview has been reduced to rubble.

It is a hole that will never really close again. It is the first of many holes—rabbit holes down into another reality—that will lead me eventually to the *dharma*, and to Rinpoche.

Traumatized by the enormity of this event, most of us think about little else for at least a year. We replay the scenario endlessly and from every conceivable angle, looking for the clue that will resolve the mystery. We cut classes to hear visiting lectures by any conspiracy theorist who comes to the campus, however demagogic or bizarre.

None of us believes the official, sanitized version of Kennedy's assassination. It is the first of many outrages over the next ten years. It begins the inevitable process of driving our whole generation to permanent distrust of our government.

Ironically, it also gives us a real sense of purpose. We feel the excitement of having something worthy to do battle against with all our strength and self-righteousness. We are now the honest young men trying to get to the bottom of the lies of the old men.

The dramatic tension seems especially heightened at a place like Yale, because we all recognize its role in the power structure we are being groomed to inherit and perpetuate.

I read *Ulysses* and take solace in Stephen Dedalus's defiant proclamation, which I underline twice: "History? History is a nightmare from which I am trying to awaken."

And then, to bring our sense of powerlessness to a breaking point, there is Vietnam.

The war in this far-off place is now on the front page of the morning paper every day. From my vantage, it seems suddenly to appear just as Kennedy disappears. From there it grows, relentless and blind as a cancer, month after month, year after year.

It shadows my time at Yale, and beyond it. It waits, malignant and implacable, for me and for my friends, in the background of our dreams and plans. It makes the rite of passage of our graduation feel futile and anticlimactic. Its unshakable presence festers in us as cynicism and helpless rage, mixed with an overpowering desire to escape.

Our poetic champion is Bob Dylan, who incandescently channels and articulates everything we feel most deeply. Behind the locked doors of our dorm rooms, his relentless genius exposes all the lies. Fiercely, he unmasks the masters of war—who order the building of the guns, shells, and bombs while hiding behind their walls and desks. He sings our righteous anger at this violent, cowardly world.

He also sings of our yearning to get as far away as we can from a world we never made and never asked for. Like a trapped alley cat looking for an exit, that haunting voice whines and wanders in a jingle-jangle morning of poignant sadness, of lonely ecstasy and release.

"Yes! Yes!"

Enraptured by Mr. Tambourine Man, we high-five each other and pass the joint 'round and 'round.

"What are you doing?" My brother is all of a sudden interrogating me with tremendous urgency.

It's an excellent question. I really have no idea. It is midsummer. I am driving very fast through the balmy night on an unlit parkway in the deep, enveloping woods of upstate New York. The convertible top of my father's car, borrowed for the day, is down. Through the radio, the Beatles sing reassuringly. We have just finished sharing a joint rolled expertly by my brother. My father has already confronted us about our new lifestyle, and after proclaiming our right to do as we please, we promise not to get high as a condition of borrowing the car. We are in a self-congratulatory mood for nothing other than being, for the moment, young and free.

Somehow, I have finished my first year at Yale …

Earlier that year, in February, the streets of New Haven are gray with icy slush, the sky an iron, unyielding gray, and the campus like a posh minimum-security prison in the middle of a Siberian waste.

A therapist is asking me what the problem seems to be. When I tell him that Kennedy has been murdered and the world is a brutal, untrustworthy place, he looks at me skeptically.

Obviously that isn't the real problem, I can almost hear him thinking. What could possibly be safer than this elite haven for spoiled rich kids? Maybe you're depressed because you've finally come to a place where everyone else is at least as smart as you, and some are even smarter. Maybe you can't bear the thought of not living up to your father's expectations. Maybe you need a girlfriend who really loves to have sex. Maybe you need to escape as soon as possible to a warm, bright beach nearer the equator.

Don't insult my intelligence, he confronts me in all but words. Tell me something real.

All these things are probably true, but the truth of the problem is deeper. I can't get to it, and I can't run away from it either …

*"Frank, what the hell are you doing?"*

My brother's sharp voice cuts through my dreamy haze. I wake up instantly.

The car I'm supposed to be driving has crossed into the oncoming lane. The lights of the approaching car are brilliant and blinding. The sound of its horn rises to a terrifying crescendo. I turn the steering wheel sharply to the right. The sound of the horn diminishes, and moments later, the red taillights vanish from my rearview mirror.

It's already over, as if I'd only dreamed it. But fear and adrenalin have brought me to a pitch of wakefulness I've never before experienced.

"Pull over!" my little brother commands like a cop.

I need no encouragement; I've already begun to guide the car to the side of the road. Moments later I'm standing in the warm, damp grass at the woods' edge, vomiting.

My brother, still nine months shy of his driver's license, turns off the radio, puts up the convertible top, and drives the remaining sixty miles home without a word. Meekly, I ask him to keep this between just the two of us for now. He nods without enthusiasm. It dawns on me then that he might be waiting for an apology for putting his life, as well as mine, at such risk.

I apologize. He focuses, without expression, on the highway ahead.

# Chapter 4

I am twenty-one the first time I visit California, on spring break with my classmate who lives in Berkeley and whose father is a professor at the university. I board a plane in gray, rainy New Haven in the morning and am delivered miraculously into a seeming paradise beside the Pacific Ocean by mid-afternoon. It is like being torn from Kansas and landing in Oz.

The warm sun, the clear blue air, the sparkling water of the bay flecked with whitecaps and a few white sails in the spring breeze, the profusion of brightly colored flowers in every direction, the hillsides dotted with stucco houses in pastel shades of lemon, pink, and pale green all bring enchantment. The impossibly wide highways and toll plazas and bridges—on which more cars than I've ever seen before flow effortlessly along—are aesthetically pleasing, rather than the ugly inconvenience I'm so used to in New York and New Haven. Even automobile exhaust seems to smell better here!

I am so utterly beguiled by the ocean atmosphere perfumed with the happy scent of all those flowers that it intoxicates me. I float through a honeysuckle world.

My classmate reneges on his promise to show me the California coast, instead holing up for the entire holiday in the university library to work on his thesis. Is he insane, I wonder? I try to dissuade him, but he is set in his purpose. No doubt he never intended to accompany me. I feel tricked and abandoned. But in retrospect, he couldn't possibly have done me a bigger favor.

No choice but to show *myself* the California coast. Incredibly, I hitchhike for several days without a moment of doubt or fear. My youth, the time—hippies in the streets of San Francisco, marijuana everywhere, the existential banner of "Make Love, Not War" in the air—I ride a wave of naïve but unshakable confidence. Indeed, it is the same insouciance that will lead me to take 1,000 micrograms of LSD less than two months later.

I'm utterly free of hesitation, and every driver who carries me along to the next way station seems easy and gentle and delighted to meet me.

Especially Paula. She is twenty-eight, beautiful, a flight attendant who likes D. H. Lawrence and Mozart and Henry Miller. She picks me up near Big Sur, takes me off the highway, and keeps me for a while. Gladly am I kept! Like Ulysses in Calypso's cave, I temporarily lose all memory of home. She rents a cabin for us in the woods near the Pacific and we spend the better part of a full week together in bed.

After so many of my fumbling adolescent experiments with high school sweethearts, college girlfriends, Friday-night New Haven pickups, even a brazen female professor who seduced me with what I anticipated would be her vast experience and then turned out to be a virgin who asked me to teach *her*—it is Paula who really opens the world of sex to me for the first time.

After the first day we hardly bother to walk to the main lodge for meals. Nothing but time and tenderness, odor of honeysuckle, bright red bougainvillea framing our window, moist curtains of fog in the deep green branches of the fir trees outside our little cabin door, and the restless sound of the great ocean on the rocky beach hundreds of feet below. All my senses heightened, so relaxed and alive. Thank you, Paula, thank you …

"What do you mean, you may not come back to the East Coast?" my father exclaims, forcefully and incredulously, into the phone.

I'm standing in a phone booth on a steep hill in San Francisco at the end of that week. I am high on sex and the sea and the red flowers and the transparency of the light and my newly discovered freedom. The prospect of returning to that cold, damp world of black and white feels almost like a prison sentence.

"You have less than three months to go before you graduate," he shouts into the receiver. "Don't be insane!"

I hang up on him.

But that evening I consider that I am not the one who's paid the huge bill and painstakingly invested in my future for the past four years. It occurs to me in that moment of sober reflection that freedom is not merely an emotion. The next day, I return to New Haven.

"The Prince got married here," Mac whispers.

I seem to be a bit confused already. What is he talking about? Who is the Prince?

Oh yes, then I remember. That's Bob's honorific title when he's playing blues on Saturday nights in New Haven with his band. Prince La La and the Midnight Creepers. It is an homage perhaps to the King himself—B. B. King, that is, whose music Bob reveres, and which he studies with far more diligence and passion than he devotes to any of his academic courses.

The Prince. It's the perfect moniker for this self-appointed apprentice and would-be heir to the King himself. Even a white boy can plausibly imagine such possibilities here at Yale—this spawning ground for future Masters of the Universe in any and all fields of dreams.

We're standing in a church on the corner of the Old Campus on a perfect late afternoon in spring. An hour ago—was it really only an hour ago?—I was riding a bus back from the baseball fields at the edge of town, gazing idly through the window at the fresh green leaves of the elms and maples along the safe, familiar avenues of New Haven. Thinking: *Only three more weeks before I leave this cloister, this gilded cage.* It's an intoxicating prospect. Relaxed and slightly dreamy, I ride the bus. My final papers are all in progress. The situation is well in hand.

It turns out to be the very last moment of my childhood.

Somehow, and without a ticket, I've transferred from that bus to another vehicle altogether—a magic sailing ship on which I will soon lose my grip entirely on whatever I previously believed to be real about my life and the world.

When exactly did this happen? I struggle to remember. Ah yes, while riding that bus I caught sight of Mac and the Prince strolling on Elm with their familiar air of carefree insouciance, knew instantly that they were high, and leaped off at the earliest opportunity to join them. The allure of the Prince and his retinue is irresistible. The man is only 21, yet already married, already with the responsibility of a baby; living off campus with his sexy wife and not on campus like the rest of us with our horny roommates; a musician with his own band, stoned much of the time; yet handling all of it and his classes too with apparent ease and ready in a few weeks—like myself but seemingly with much less hard work—to graduate with honors.

In our rarefied little world this is the most exalted achievement—to do everything perfectly with little or no discernible effort. And beyond even that, to be playfully contemptuous of it all at the same time. It's the supreme accomplishment for a Yalie. The Prince! A truly awesome figure in a realm where everyone else can only hope to be someday worthy of awe.

The offering is slightly unfamiliar this time—not the usual joint, but a small white pill. Without a moment's pause, I swallow it. After all, it's a beautiful day. And after all, these are my friends. My blood brothers, even!

Years later, my mother speculates gravely:

"Don't you think those classmates of yours were being paid by the CIA to conduct tests on students who were actively opposed to the war? Don't you think they were setting you up?"

"I doubt it, Mom. I really doubt it. But it's an interesting thought."

"I've read that things like that were going on then at colleges all over the country."

"I suppose it's possible. But it's pretty unlikely, Mom."

"Well, I will always think it was something like that. No

one is going to persuade me otherwise." She says this with humorless finality, as if we were sitting together reading the obituary of a third person who'd been a friend of mine, some young man who died before his life ever really began. I think of her handsome brother, lost over China.

The light of late New Haven afternoon streams like wine through the rich red stained-glass windows of the church. The air in the cavernous interior is dark and cool, but the light coming through that high, floating window is like a warm bath of colors. Little rainbows begin to dance on the stone floor. The Prince stands there in his own lordly and solitary reverie.

Did Mac just say something to me?

Certainly he is looking at me now—peering at me, really. I see him whisper something to the Prince behind the now slightly ominous screen of his long, lank black hair, but I can't quite make any of it out.

My mood shifts abruptly and utterly, without my volition, as if my psychic temperature has just dropped forty degrees in an instant. Around the edges of the rainbow pool where the Prince and Mac are standing, the floor of the old church is black and cold. The angels I thought I saw moments ago have vanished, and I really don't want to be here anymore.

I leave the church. They follow closely behind. Too closely, it feels.

"You didn't take the whole thing, did you?"

"Yes, I did."

"He took the whole thing, Bob."

Where are we now? What time is it?

Words do not form easily, and when they are about to

form, they dissolve and slide away before they can be spoken. B. B. King is playing, beckoning from a still-familiar world that is rapidly receding from view, and reminding me uncannily that the thrill is gone, and gone away for good.

I have not been in this room before. Is this the living room of the Prince's apartment? The others are sitting around a green table in the room, listening to the King.

There's a big knife on the table, a kitchen knife. Why is there a knife on that table? Relax, there's a wedge of bright yellow cheese next to the knife. Mac is raising a glass of red and smiling with large stained teeth. Mac the Knife. That wedge of cheese is so yellow. I am mesmerized by a red circle next to a yellow triangle on a larger green circle. So that's what colors are ... And who are these people, anyway?

Again the light. Like that light in the church before. Now it draws me from a window across this room with the knife in it. So bright there at the window, so much darker where these strangers are sitting. I move toward that light. Moth to the flame. Through the open window the late afternoon air is soothing. A tender breeze stirs the leaves of a single sycamore in the velvet street below. Across the street a red brick facade begins to melt in the rich but fading sunlight. Is it the sunlight or is it the bricks that have now become deep red-orange honey pouring from a giant bottle all over my field of vision?

B. B. King's voice and the honey-colored brick-sunlight have become inseparable parts of a single experience of melting. I am now nothing other than the kaleidoscopic flow of all these sensations. I have become the music, the light, the temperature of the breeze. I cannot find anything of me now that is not this exquisite, pulsing field of direct perception. My own body dissolves ecstatically into this field, and without thought of anyone or anything else, I begin to dance.

I look down at my legs. Are they really *my* legs? They are impossibly long, like stretched taffy, like a figure out of El Greco's overactive imagination ascending to some lurid Castilian heaven. These legs pulse like a thousand beehives as they move on the gleaming hardwood floor of the room with that big knife on the round green table.

The others are looking at me again. They are looking at me strangely. Why are none of them dancing? Why am I the only one dancing? Why is there a knife on that table?

> And all who heard should see him there
> And all should cry Beware! Beware!
> His flashing eyes, his floating hair!
>
> (Samuel Taylor Coleridge, "Kubla Khan")

It is deep night now. That honeyed sun set aeons ago. And words have long since become useless, inaccessible.

Two extremes alternate with growing intensity and rapidity. In one moment I am inseparable from everyone and everything else, and words become redundant. The overwhelming reality of our sharing this astonishing, luminous field of perception is so complete and self-evident that verbal confirmation is unnecessary. Nor could words ever begin to encompass such an experience.

In the next moment, I am utterly separate from everyone else, and they in turn are utterly separate from one another. We are like cold blue stars pulsing alone in a vast, barren universe. Now words are utterly futile, since the abyss between each of us is so unbridgeable. It is as if anything we speak is an undeliverable message, blown away into the void the moment it is spoken. And without words, the bottom of our mutually agreed-upon world falls out. The loneliness of these black hours is terrifying and endless. Will day never come again?

We're approaching the Tomb now, the place where our Secret Society meets each Thursday evening. It is one of perhaps half a dozen venerable fortresses scattered like dragon's teeth on the edge of the Yale campus. It is a massive granite monolith without windows. Each of us has a key to the single giant, heavy front door. Ivy grows profusely through the crevices between the orderly blocks of stone, garlanding the top of the massive door. The real Ivy League, indeed! Our Tomb and our Secret Society, where we future Masters of the Universe assemble each week for the purpose of ...

*"Skull and Bones! Accept or Reject?"*

One year before, on a balmy night in May much like this one, two upperclassmen in tuxedoes stood stiffly at attention like sentries at my dorm door, looking at me sternly and awaiting my reply. But I'd been waiting for them too, armed with the rumors I'd heard of coffins; of wrestling in the mud; of being beaten up and thrown into one of those coffins, then to rise and be reborn as a Bonesman in all his glory; of homoerotic elitism; of half FDR's and JFK's cabinets having been Bonesmen, even though they themselves were Harvard men; of guarantees of ten thousand dollars a year for the rest of your life whether you'd ended up a struggling artist or a comfortable captain of industry, a multi-millionaire or a pauper.

Who really knew whether any of this was true if they hadn't actually been Bonesmen themselves? Certainly these two elegant stiffs standing implacably in front of my dormitory door weren't giving anything away.

*"Reject!"*

More frightened than seduced by all the lurid stories, I turned down Skull and Bones, much to the astonishment of my classmates. Yet I went on to join another Secret Society instead. The peer pressure at this level of privilege was too great to resist …

The door of our fraternal Tomb rises up before me, as ominous as an approaching tank. I turn in terror and run across the empty avenue into the welcoming darkness of the neighboring cemetery.

The grass is damp and cool as I throw myself down among the marble headstones. The silent presence of the dead in every direction is oddly comforting. I am one of them now—a member of the ultimate secret society. I feel my feverish face tickled gently by every soft black blade of grass. I press my head against the earth, longing to sink into it, to bury my body in its soothing embrace …

Twenty-five years later, a classmate approaches me under the jauntily striped blue-and-white tent of our class reunion. I struggle to remember his name to introduce him to my wife.

"Do you remember that night when you were wandering around the New Haven cemetery stoned out of your mind and we kept trying to get you back into the car?

"We all thought you'd gone off the deep end for good that night," he adds with a laugh. The ice cubes in his drink tinkle against the side of the glass.

"Yeah, I suppose I did."

Amazing he still remembered this. Was he actually there that night? Why didn't I remember him? Who else was there, I wonder. My fifteen minutes of fame. And what is even more amazing—how with enough time anything can seem funny–proof of the old saw that comedy is just tragedy plus time. The man moves on, drink in hand, sparing me the awkward introductions …

Mac the Knife is pulling me back across the avenue and up the stony path again, toward the Tomb, toward the Death in Life again. Of course, the Tomb! That's our connection! That has always been my connection with Mac the Knife and the Prince of Darkness. We were total strangers before we met at the Tomb, and we're total strangers now.

The top of Kennedy's head is gone, and rich old Bonesmen are sending poor, young uninitiated men across the oceans to die so that this great bronze ivied door can stand till the end of time. The end of time … Suddenly there is nothing but brilliant white light, overpowering and all pervasive. It's not coming from anywhere outside me. No, it *is* me. No longer able to think at all now, no longer able to find my body anywhere. There is just the light. There is just the light, and also a penetrating intuition that this experience is final in some way. It is final not only in the sense of being the end for the person I have always identified as "myself," but also in the sense that there is clearly nothing beyond this experience that my mind could even have.

> And to die is different from what any one supposed …
>
> (Walt Whitman, "Song of Myself")

Then an image flickers behind or inside this light as my mind tumbles down into self-consciousness once again. Family and friends have gathered in a ring—my parents, my brothers and sisters, my best friends from childhood, my roommates at Yale. They are all gazing at me with kindness and concern as I sit meekly in the center of their circle.

I'm sure I hear my father say, "He's not coming back. Who did this to my son?"

I try to speak, but there are no words to be had. Then a still, small witness—all that I can now salvage of the sanity I must have had before this terrifying ride began—observes with surprising equanimity, even humor, how arbitrary it all is that he could have lost his mind in this way. Just a little pill without thinking, but then again, he was always a bit impulsive, not all that grounded sometimes.

I want to tell them all that it's okay. That if I know I've lost my mind then perhaps I haven't lost it after all.

This is not the first time this still, clear, slightly ironic voice has announced its presence this night. Reflecting on it later, it will assume a growing, even an uncanny significance. Then the lurid, torrential river of thoughts, feelings, and images sweeps me onward once more …

It is just before dawn. I have mysteriously rematerialized a block from the spot where I got off the bus twelve hours ago, thrown up again onto the shore of my old life like a piece of luggage from a shipwreck. It seems I have lived several lifetimes since leaving that bus yesterday.

In the dorm bathroom sink I submerge my head in cold water, as if to wash all traces of the terror I have just endured. As I look into the mirror above it, my own face begins to morph effortlessly into that of my father, my mother, my brothers and sister. Simply recalling them makes them appear instantly in place of my own reflection.

At first I am intrigued by this magical trick of perception, then touched and slowly overcome by a profound sense of love and gratitude and connection. I am alive. I am back. This is my life this time. This is my family this time. This time. It is all so obvious and so clear. I look into the bathroom mirror again, and there's no reflection at all. I will the reflection to come back, and it does.

I look in on my roommate as he sleeps. We've roomed together for four years, yet now I feel as if I'm seeing him for the first time. The curly hair he's endlessly trying to straighten before Vassar women arrive for weekend parties—as he sleeps it falls in chaotic profusion around his face and over his pillow. How beautiful he looks! I have an impulse to wake him and tell him he looks like an angel. Mercifully, I stifle it and let him sleep.

I walk outside. My whole being is calm, soft, tender, and relaxed. By now the sun has fully risen. No one else in the world is stirring. Every leaf, flower, and blade of grass, every stone, bird, and squirrel, every crawling creature is suffused with vivid light. The whole world is made of light, and the sharp boundaries of all these forms relax and dissolve. I seem to understand at this moment, beyond even the slightest flicker of doubt, that all boundaries are the creations of thought, which divides what has never been separate.

And the light that is now shining on things is also shining from within things; these outer and inner lights seem to dance together in one perfect, radiant display. The color and light in the paintings of Monet and Van Gogh, or the countless tiny dots of brilliant color Seurat used to create the illusion of form, even these most exquisite representations of nature by artists of unquestionable genius—which I have always loved—cannot begin to approach the splendor of the luminous reality directly before my eyes this mild May morning on an ordinary street in New Haven.

> Weave a circle round him thrice,
> And close your eyes with holy dread,
> For he on honey-dew hath fed
> And drunk the milk of Paradise.
>
> ("Kubla Khan")

Finally, in the face of this vision of perfection, I feel such sadness for all the suffering that I and all other human beings have experienced and all that we will experience in the future. I am awed at the depths of pain into which I have just descended, and grateful that I have somehow been permitted to return to this world.

I do not know what I will make of the rest of my life any more than I knew twelve hours before, but I know something profound in me has shifted irrevocably—and that whatever I do, it must somehow reflect and express this change. There is no way back to the innocent dreamer who got off that bus yesterday afternoon.

It has dawned on me fully for the first time that heaven and hell do truly exist, and that they are within the mind, and nowhere else. But it has not yet begun to occur to me that, in their very essence, *they are exactly the same.*

It will take a master warrior teacher to show me that. And I still don't even know that I'm looking for him.

The situation reminds me of my favorite joke about spirituality:

*What's the difference between a mystic and a psychotic?*

*The only difference is who they decide to tell about their experience.*

That was my dilemma at the time. The experience of that night had been life-changing in ways that I had not even begun to fully appreciate or comprehend.

At the same time, in retrospect, I have no doubt that it was a psychotic break. It had been artificially but decisively induced by a hallucinogenic substance, taken in excessive dosage without proper preparation or guidance.

Getting stoned was one thing; losing my mind for twelve hours was another altogether.

As I began to research—both through reading and anecdotally—I found that more than a few others had had this kind of experience and not returned from it. Ever. I shivered at the seeming arbitrariness of life and fate and muttered a silent prayer of thanksgiving at my relative good fortune.

Certainly many intuitive breakthroughs occurred. In the moment of their occurrence they were—like so much else of that long, long night—utterly beyond words to express. But as the experience settled, and as I began to educate myself for the first time in the teachings of mystics and spiritual masters both ancient and modern, Eastern and Western, some basic insights began to become clear to me. I developed what can only be described as irrefutable confidence in them, despite the fact that I would never—then or even now—have any demonstrable, objective proof for any of them.

First, that I create my world with my thoughts. This creation is my "trip," and it is ultimately up to me—and no one else—what trip I decide to take with my life. It is the mind, and the mind alone, that creates heaven and hell. Ultimately, they are the overpoweringly vivid reflections of my mental fixation—nothing more, and nothing less.

At the same time, there seems to be some unchanging and indestructible essence in my being that has no beginning or end, and is not dependent on the elements of my personality. That is, it is not dependent on thought. This seemingly indestructible essence—call it "the witness" or "the knower" if you like—is not altered or affected even by the death of my body. It is not limited in space by the apparent boundary of my body, or limited in time by the apparent reality of the drama of "this life," with all its hopes and fears.

Apart from this truth of being, there is no God in any external sense, and there never has been. As a consequence, there are also no transcendental guarantees or confirmations for this lonely journey I am making. There is no cosmic parent taking care of my life script.

I am truly alone in the universe. But depending upon how I relate to this truth, it may be a source of panic, isolation, and despair on the one hand, or peace, connection, and completeness on the other—because the universe is inseparable from my being.

There is no freedom beyond this. All other expressions of freedom that human beings proclaim are either partial (think: philosophy) or dishonest (think: politics) or both. Words are always inadequate and misleading in describing all this because of their inherent dualism. Using one word for one thing and another word for another already insists on their separateness rather than their inseparability: that this is *this*, and that is *that*. Yet we need words to communicate with others—others who are confused and suffering because of their confusion—even if the words provide only shadowy approximations for the phenomena to which they refer.

In this sense, the supreme value of words is their function as a gesture of compassion. I would learn later that this is what the Buddha meant when he referred to his teachings—the *dharma*—as being like a finger pointing to the moon. The moon represents the ultimate experience of knowing, whereas the finger is simply the verbal description. Again and again, he warned, "Do not mistake the finger for the moon."

It is interesting to reflect upon how many of the spiritual traditions that rely almost entirely on their Book as the ultimate repository of wisdom end up trapped in a world of dogma, even to the point where their adherents are willing to fight and kill others with opposing views in order to protect the "sacredness" of their own Book. This is a particularly poignant example of the mistake of confusing the finger for the moon.

It is said the Buddha himself faced this conundrum just after he attained enlightenment. Perhaps he found himself reflecting along the following lines:

"What I have experienced is profound and wondrous, but if I try to tell others, they will probably not believe me. I should probably stay here in the forest and continue to meditate for the rest of my life.

"On the other hand, perhaps if I don't try to come up with some heavy-handed, systematic philosophical trip in advance and then go out and lay it on people, there might be some other way to communicate that will reach them directly.

"Maybe I should just get up from my meditation seat under this tree and start walking. I'll simply relate directly with whomever I meet and with whatever situations I encounter along the way.

"If I've learned anything true or helpful to others, then what I've learned should speak for itself. If not, there's no use in making a nuisance of myself. There are already so many charlatans out there peddling spirituality. Why add to the mess?

"I'll just start walking, and see what happens. At this point, I certainly don't have anything better to do."

He started walking. And he kept walking, and teaching, for forty years.

He was not, by the way, the Buddha yet. He was still Siddhartha Gautama. The meaning of the word *buddha* is simply "the one who is awake." It wasn't something he called himself, but rather a name others gave him when they encountered him, saw and felt his presence, and heard what he had to say. It was obvious to everyone who met him that he was fully and completely awake to the truth of how things are. And because of this, all who met him were powerfully drawn to him.

The Buddha did teach with words of course. But even more, he taught with his actions and gestures. And most of all, he taught with his overwhelming authentic presence, which embodied and communicated a truth beyond the trap or the mirage of words. In this way, he never limited himself to the authority of the Book, nor did he instruct his followers to do so.

The truth of his realization spoke for itself. Like that of the Buddha I myself would fall in love with, seven years later.

# Chapter 5

My father's hair seems to turn white overnight that summer. Maybe it's just his biological clock. But more likely, it's me.

Whatever else my drug experience two months earlier has been, it certainly is not a sudden inspiration to teach anyone else about the meaning of life. I plummet into depression. Somehow I finish the remaining weeks of college and cross the stage with my Yale diploma like everyone else, but the accomplishment feels hollow and meaningless.

The one photograph remaining from that occasion shows a smiling young man with thick, unruly dark brown hair in broad June sunlight, wearing blue cap and gown in an ocean of blue caps and gowns. My father is proud that day, no doubt, but probably more relieved than anything else. I am dazed.

What will I do next? Never mind for the rest of my life—how about just for the coming summer? I am listless, without motivation, ready to be pushed in any direction by anyone who has a plan more definite than my own, no matter how questionable or misguided it might be.

My classmate Drew has just such a plan. Let's go to a seaside town on Cape Cod, rent a house there, get jobs as waiters, make lots of money, read poetry, drink, and pick up women at night. It's a time-honored plan, requiring no imagination or vision, simply youthful male hormones.

Drew has these in abundance, along with an entrepreneurial vigor that is relentless. He'll put up the deposit for the house we find, take on the responsibility for renting out the extra rooms, and assume the risks and rewards for whatever the situation yields by summer's end. All I'm required to do is pick out a nice room for myself on the top floor and bring my favorite books of poetry with me. Like flotsam on the tide, I drift along in the wake of his enthusiasm.

The plan is complicated slightly by the fact that the town of choice turns out to be Provincetown—the gay mecca of the Eastern seaboard at the time. Drew has been reading Eugene O'Neill all semester and wants to spend the summer in the place where he wrote some of his masterpieces. A budding young playwright in his own right, Drew rhapsodizes about a windswept house on the beach, surrounded by the picturesque, turbulent Atlantic waves that will inspire him to great depths of existential insight.

But it turns out he's more actor than dramatist, the truth being that he really only wants to get laid, nor is he overly discriminating about gender. I watch him with a mixture of curiosity and grudging admiration.

We settle for a more pedestrian location than O'Neill did—a rooming house on the main street of town, a few hundred yards from the notorious Meat Rack, where gay men cruise each other every night. Within a week, Drew has rented the three remaining rooms out to a motley assortment of drugged-out young drifters from Boston. When I point out to him that one of them appears to be using methamphetamine and another to be peddling it, he breezily assures me that they're good for the rent so far, and that as long as they keep paying on time and keep to themselves, he sees no problem.

Besides, he reminds me, it's his financial risk, not mine. I should relax and enjoy my summer. He will take care of the inconvenient, nitty-gritty details. I let him flatter me, and avert my eyes.

The truth of the matter is that I'm too depressed to put up any more than the most token resistance. In its aftermath, the long night of drug-induced psychosis—despite the ecstatic overtones of its final hour— stays with me as a sense of hopelessness, a condition of enervation that seems more deep than merely psychological, but somatic as well. For the first time in my life, I do not look forward to getting out of bed in the morning.

I soon find myself enmeshed in a cocooned liaison with a lovely but almost equally despondent young lady who spends much of her time each day painting empty colored bottles with endlessly repeated patterns of tiny daisy petals. We hide out together in my room most of the summer. Drew begins going to the Meat Rack, and often sleeps elsewhere. Downstairs, our boarders get high.

I go to work each afternoon at a popular restaurant and make good tips, though they're nothing like what Drew is raking in. His insouciant willingness to flirt with every rich gay man who comes to dinner there is invariably lucrative.

Late each evening I return to my room, put the cash in an envelope in the top drawer of my bureau, listen to my girlfriend play hopeful folk songs on her guitar by candlelight, lean over the bed we are sharing to kiss her goodnight, then leave the house to pace on the beach alone in the darkness for hours. I think of little but suicide. I share these despairing thoughts with no one but myself. My loneliness and self-absorption are profound.

When I return to the house from these doleful excursions, our other tenants are invariably sitting at the kitchen table, passing a joint. With the easy, indiscriminate friendliness of stoned hippies, they invite me to join them. I smile and decline, and go back upstairs to bed.

I dread the rising of the sun next morning, but drag myself from my bed nevertheless, and do the whole thing all over again.

There is a well-known saying that ignorance of the law is no excuse. This seems to apply not only to legal violations, but to deeper karmic ones as well. My state of mind seems to be held in a kind of stupefied suspension by my wish for the world to stop just long enough for me to get off it for a while. I convince myself that this is what I'm doing. I'm like a child who puts his hand over his eyes and then believes that everything he was just looking at has ceased to exist.

By early August, our housemate downstairs—a charming bisexual con man from Montreal—is openly dealing out of his room. Drew is gone most of the time now from what has become a local drug haven. My girlfriend's father, a career naval officer with ramrod posture and unshakable Christian morals, has come to take her out of this den of iniquity. She has meekly gone along with him.

I should recognize all the warning signs then and there. But somehow impervious to all of these changes, I plod aimlessly along, as if simply getting through the summer in this place would be a major life accomplishment of some kind.

One evening after work, I return to find the house full of cops. Everyone downstairs is being led away in a paddy wagon. A policeman asks me my name and whether I live there; foolishly I answer honestly on both counts instead of invoking my rights. He produces an airmail envelope with my name and address on it; inside it is a small quantity of marijuana.

Incredibly, I have left this in my room, in the drawer next to the envelope with the cash.

I have not even used any of it and, after the trauma in New Haven two months earlier, have no real intention of doing so. My embarrassment at my stupidity outweighs even my shame at being arrested. About the ownership of the grass, at least I have the presence of mind to remain silent.

I spend the night in the town jail. By the next morning, my father has driven two hundred miles to bail me out. Again and again he shakes his head. What has happened to his oldest son, his rising star, his pride and joy? His sadness and disappointment are almost unbearable to witness. I give him all of my hard-earned cash, telling him it will help with the lawyer I will obviously need right away. He gives it back, saying I should keep it because I've earned it and will need it later for other things.

I marvel that he can still maintain a vision of my life possibilities that extends beyond the next twenty-four hours. My feelings of being unworthy of his unswerving love are very difficult to hold. Thoughts of suicide scream inside my head.

After the local judge finds me guilty of possession of marijuana, my father drives to Boston to hire the best lawyer he can afford. The lawyer is a big, confident man with a rough-hewn face that reminds me of photos of Lincoln and an easy familiarity with the law in such cases. Never for a moment does he express any doubt that the local judge's verdict will not hold up on appeal, an attitude that greatly heartens my father, if not myself.

Six weeks later, the original conviction is overturned on procedural grounds. The police used a faulty search warrant. The legal blot is quickly expunged from my permanent record. My father breathes freely again. I am still too numb to care, or to appreciate the irony that the very privilege I despise is there for me to take advantage of whenever I really need it. And it is not altogether comforting to realize how much more invested my father is in my own life at this point than I am.

It is a year after my graduation from Yale. I'm living in New York. The apartment where I reside and the school where I work are placed like acupuncture points at the far ends of the central meridian of Atlantic Avenue—the great artery that runs from one end of Brooklyn to the other. The geographical distance is less than five miles. But as for the cultural, economic, and existential gap between those two points, Atlantic Avenue might just as well be the Atlantic Ocean.

I have a small apartment in Brooklyn Heights, near the promenade on which I walk briskly early each morning before descending into the subway. I can smell the air of the harbor, watch the great cargo ships move in and out of the port, feel the sweep of the Brooklyn Bridge, with its graceful cables truly like the harp strings which Hart Crane celebrated, and gaze at the arrogant, implacable skyline of Lower Manhattan and Wall Street.

I am working in what can only be called Brooklyn Depths—the Ocean Hill-Brownsville ghetto, where I try to teach poor young children, mostly black, to read and write. Teaching here is one of several alternatives to being sent to Vietnam. At least one of my friends has chosen each of the others, so I'm familiar with them all.

I could escape to Canada and not return for a while—if ever. I could get a medical deferment from the military by pretending to be crazy—in my own case not so far-fetched after my drug experience the previous year. I could apply for conscientious objector status on moral or religious grounds.

To begin with, I investigate this third option, but I'm told in advance that my application will be denied because I have no formal religious affiliation or church to support it. Someone on the draft board knows my father—more than likely as the doctor who takes care of his children. It is not until years later that I even consider the level of personal privilege implied in the simple fact that I can get a definitive ruling about being a C.O. from my draft board without having to actually risk applying.

So here I am, teaching poor, black people in America as an alternative to killing poor, yellow people in Asia. "Alternative service deferment" is the official category for what I'm doing here. Later, I joke at times that going to Vietnam might have been safer. But I realize, too, that this work is just the medicine I need to free myself from my state of paralyzed self-absorption.

My first day at P.S. 178K can only be described as hallucinatory. Almost half a dozen of the thirty new teachers who show up for work at that elementary school—all of them there for precisely the same reason as myself—are personal friends from the full range of my own school experiences: David from lower school, Peter from middle school, Mike from high school, Barry from college.

It is shocking to see the power of this war to determine the life choices of my entire generation—overprivileged refugees seeking shelter, livelihood, and useful service. None of us would have willingly and freely chosen such work as a career, given our other options. And none of us even stop to consider, probably, the extent of our good fortune that we can slide so easily for the time being into this relatively safe harbor from the violence of the war.

Yet the neighborhood around the school looks itself like a war zone under aerial bombardment. In every direction are dilapidated buildings with missing windows and crumbling walls. Whole blocks have been ravaged by fire and not rebuilt. Sidewalks are littered with garbage and rivers of broken glass from empty bottles of cheap wine and whiskey. Local drug potentates deal openly from doorways. Junkies and drunks stumble in and out of vacant storefronts, blinking in the bright sunlight like creatures who have lived in the darkness for aeons.

From this broken world each morning, like some kind of miraculous phoenix rising from its own ashes, come the youth, the nine- and ten-year-olds. Scrubbed clean from ear to ear and then dressed in cheap but neatly pressed clothing by their indomitable mothers, dutifully carrying their books and their lunch boxes (and with their mothers keeping a watchful eye from the sidewalk), they file through the gate in the barbed-wire fence that surrounds the school as the morning bell buzzes harshly over the cracked concrete yard.

The stairs they climb to their classrooms might just as well be the hill up which Sisyphus pushes his rock. Relatively speaking, the girls' situation is certainly more hopeful than the boys'. No matter how privileged the culture, boys are slower to develop. But here, the gap is especially startling. The whole culture has become a matriarchy by attrition. Mothers run the community and their daughters learn to become their able lieutenants by the time they are nine. The fathers are absent—a whole generation decimated by lack of schooling, by unemployment, drugs, alcohol, violence, hopelessness.

These they pass on to the sons, with few exceptions.

The girls rule the classrooms. They are far more disciplined, more sensible, more eager, and better readers. Brenda, Sylista, and Johnnie Mae lead the class in every subject.

The boys lag. They are wild, sullen, clueless about the world that awaits them, and channel all their man-child energies into fighting with each other, both in the classroom and outside it. For James, Miles, Robert, and Alphonso—all of them bewildered young warriors—the English words in the class textbook might just as well be Egyptian hieroglyphics.

Incredibly, the books are just like the ones *I* read in elementary school. Worn and tattered, they may well *be* the very books I read in grade school, remaindered out to these children after they'd outlived their usefulness to white children. A white world, where Dick, Jane, Sally, and their dog Spot romp together in leafy green suburban neighborhoods with perfect white picket fences enclosing each orderly little square of lawn.

Naturally, there is nothing in these books to which these children can relate in any way. Even if they could read the words in them—which the vast majority cannot do—the airbrushed world to which the words refer is utterly alien to them, mocking the harsh truth of their world at every turn.

What to do?

I soon learn that these children have no interest or intention of trying to learn to read by means of these books, and that their attention and imagination are being held hostage perpetually by the world they have just left behind. Next to what they experience in the sixteen hours each day they are not in my presence, I have no real, vivid world to offer them as an alternative.

Then it dawns on me that the only way I will ever teach them to read and write is to let them have full access to their own world. I collect their textbooks, put them all in a box, and put the box in the classroom closet. In my two years there, we will not open those books again.

I ask them to tell me stories about their lives. At first they simply relate them aloud in front of their classmates. One story inspires another. They compete at times to see who can shock their white-boy teacher the most. The line between reality and lurid fantasy is blurred. I know I'm being conned at times, but maintain one rule of conduct at every turn—and that is, to be unfailingly interested in whatever any child may be telling me in the moment of the telling.

Then we begin to shift from oral to written mode. I tell them to begin writing their stories down. The girls go to it eagerly; the boys complain that they don't know how to spell any of the words they want to write. I tell them to call out the words they want to know how to spell and I will write them on the blackboard.

At this point the room begins to buzz with a loud, chaotic, but relentlessly purposeful energy—like a commodities exchange. From every corner come the urgent, questioning calls: "junkies," "fire engines," "smack," "dollars," "mother." Everyone has a story to tell, and everyone has words to spell. Within an hour, the big blackboard at the front of the shabby classroom is covered with words, and the lined paper in front of each child is covered with words as well—the words of his or her story for that morning.

At the end of class, I collect the papers and correct each of them for grammar, spelling, and punctuation. In the afternoon, I return them and the children rewrite them so that they are impeccable. Then each child adds the paper to his or her folder—a portfolio of finished work.

I remember the energy and joy of breaking down the barriers between their world and mine in that hour each morning. I remember their growing confidence in being able to express their life experiences with written words. I remember their dignity in being able to give voice to even the most painful and horrific aspects of their lives and see them written down clearly and cleanly in the pages of their folders, as if in doing so they gained some measure of control over their worlds. I remember, most of all, our mutual pleasure and even gratitude at listening and being listened to.

This is all I remember now of my time teaching these poor, young children. Even at the time, I had no illusions that what I was doing there would have a lasting, transformative effect on their lives. I had no idea whether any of them would ever finish high school or go to college. I had no doubt that some of the boys in my class would not survive until adulthood. But of course, I never received confirmation for any of my suppositions. After my two years there, I never saw any of them again.

One incident from that time stands out with special poignancy. In my many, shifting roles with these children—teacher, impresario, father figure, comforter, disciplinarian, warden, judge—this moment brings into sharpest focus my essential and underlying powerlessness in the face of the stubborn enormity of the challenges of their world.

Two boys suddenly begin fighting in the back of the classroom. Verbal taunts have quickly escalated into a full-blown confrontation of vicious kicks and punches. The class has instantly become a bloodthirsty crowd at a cockfight, and my status as venerable word wizard has degenerated in a flash into that of ineffectual referee.

I rush to the back of the class to break up the fight. In the process, a wild punch thrown by one at the other hits me in the jaw. I separate the two of them and begin the futile but obligatory ritual of trying to determine who was at fault—not to punish them, but to compel the aggressor to apologize in front of the rest of the class.

I stand there, holding them apart as they continue to flail at each other. If they were any older, I would not have the strength to separate them. My jaw is sore and I can taste blood inside my mouth. Later, I will discover that this blind blow from a nine-year-old has knocked out one of my back teeth.

"Who started this?" I demand sternly, conscious even as I do of the impotence of my position.

The ring of cheering children shouts out a whole range of passionate opinions. The two combatants stare at each other, fierce and unrepentant. Finally, unable to sort out any clear story from this screaming maelstrom, I command each of them to apologize to the other.

They balk. I glower. They give in, sort of.

"Sorry," mutters one.

"Sorry didn't do it," replies the other. And nothing will persuade or compel him to say another word of contrition or explanation beyond this.

*Sorry didn't do it.*

Forty years later, these words echo in my memory as the final summation, the very essence of the meaning of my whole experience in Ocean Hill-Brownsville.

Sorry didn't do it. "Sorry" didn't cause this pain. Other human beings and their unresponsive institutions caused this pain, generation after generation.

Sorry didn't do it. Even more deeply, "sorry" is not an adequate response or answer in the face of this pain. Sorry doesn't do it. Sorry just doesn't cut it, man.

During my first year teaching in that ghetto, Martin Luther King, Jr. and Robert Kennedy are both assassinated. In response, inner cities all over the United States go up in flames. The silent majority elects a government that it believes will protect it from the chaos of the enemy that surrounds it on all sides. Whether they imagine that enemy has a yellow face or a black one or even a white one with beards and long hair, whether it's wars or prisons that will buy them the security they demand, the silent majority has its day.

After the initial novelty and even euphoria of bringing our gifts to this forsaken world, I and my contemporaries move on as soon as we can—especially those of us who draw high draft lottery numbers the following year and no longer need fear the capricious roulette wheel of military service.

Those of us who stay longer soon outstay our welcome, as the black communities we were hired to help begin to regard us as patronizing interlopers, and exercise their new-found militancy to run their own school boards and local councils, as well they should.

Whether we leave by choice or by compulsion, we are soon gone.

Sorry didn't do it.

And sorry doesn't do it. Most deeply of all, I glimpse for the first time in my life that compassion has nothing to do with feeling sorry for other people. That compassion is simply being with the suffering, bearing witness to it, and never for a moment losing sight of the other person's humanity and dignity.

True compassion such as this requires a strength and patience well beyond my capacities at this time in my life. Still youthful, but exhausted by the depth and persistence of the suffering I witness here, I pick up my last paycheck and move on like all the others.

# Chapter 6

I develop an immediate interest in Henry David Thoreau's classic book for the first time less out of any profound connection with nature and contemplation, and more out of simple narcissism. At the age of eleven, I see an old book with my middle name, Walden, as its title in my parents' bookcase. Excited, I ask my father whether I was named after the book. He shakes his head.

"Maybe the man you were named after was named after the book; but you were named after him, and he was my roommate in medical school. His first and middle names are Frank Walden. You're his namesake.

"But it's a good book," he adds. "You should read it someday."

As time passes, and I actually read *Walden*, this lineage is not at all satisfying. I would like a more direct ancestral connection to Thoreau and his beautiful book about living alone in the woods. It is not until thirteen years later, when I am living in that tiny apartment in Brooklyn, commuting underground each day like a coal miner to the ghetto neighborhood to earn my bread as a teacher, and dreaming of trees and greenery and clear running streams, that I truly discover Thoreau, and *Walden*, for the first time:

> I went to the woods because I wished to live deliberately, to front only the essential facts of life, and see if I could not learn what it had to teach, and not, when I came to die, discover that I had not lived. I did not wish to live what was not life—living is so dear.

It is not just a change of scenery I long for, though that is certainly a constant nagging desire that has got hold of my spirit like a dog with a bone. More than that, it is the sense that I am not living the life I'm supposed to live, and that it would be a terrible thing if I were to die without ever having tried, to die as one of the mass of men who "lead lives of quiet desperation."

Now if Henry isn't talking to *me* right there, then I have no idea who he's talking to! My life in the city suffocates and exhausts me. My idealism about making a difference through political or social activism has entirely dried up. I perceive that there is just as much aggression, ambition, and vanity in that world as any other. Surely there must be a simpler, purer world. What was that vision I had at the very end of my LSD nightmare, if not the promise of such a world?

And another Henry is also nagging constantly at my restless imagination, and urging me to take action in the face of my own discontent during this time. I read Henry Miller night after night, joining my heart with his as he plots his eventual escape from his tedious, life-sucking labors at the Cosmodemonic Telephone Company, right here in Brooklyn fifty years earlier. With a contagious fearlessness, he proclaims the despair and anxiety, the absence of joy or love, the empty materialistic scramble that is life in the great city in which I now find myself living, the city of New York in which I was born.

I imagine myself as his spiritual and literary heir, as he pursues with Dionysian abandon his true vocation as a writer and a cultural revolutionary in New York and then in Paris. I am lost in dreams and the mirage of yet unrealized possibilities. Any world but the one I'm currently inhabiting will do.

The summer between my two years as a teacher in New York, I travel the United States alone in my VW squareback. The vastness and elemental beauty of the American West, after the claustrophobia of all those months commuting underground in Brooklyn, is a tonic for my spirit. To be sure, I feel lonely, but I also feel free. The open road beckons endlessly, and each morning promises a new adventure.

Halfway through that journey, I meet the woman who will become my first wife. She and her girlfriend are traveling by motorcycle across the West. Our paths intersect in the campground of the Great Sand Dunes of southern Colorado, where we have pitched our tents for the night in neighboring campsites. Preparing my evening meal, I accidentally set fire to my Coleman stove, and Marcia and her friend rush to my rescue, helping me to douse the flames. On this comically antiheroic note, our relationship begins.

By summer's end, she returns with me to Brooklyn Heights and moves in with me. I go back to Ocean Hill-Brownsville for a second year of teaching, while she finds work in a neighborhood flower shop. A talented artist in drawing, painting, and embroidery, she is a genius with flowers. Later, after we have separated, she will pursue a lifelong vocation in *ikebana*, the Japanese art of flower arranging—in which she will become a true master. For now, she adorns our tiny apartment with fresh flowers each week, and brings an ongoing air of freshness and promise into the heavy hopelessness of the ghetto world whose traces I carry home with me every evening.

The following year, the government institutes a lottery for the draft. All the days of the calendar year are drawn from a big barrel by the director of Selective Service himself. The earlier the day of your birth is chosen, the higher the odds you'll be called up for military service. Mine is the 219th to be picked, and by year's end the masters of war haven't even called number 150 yet. It is then that I decide it is safe to quit my teaching job and move with Marcia to Vermont, where her parents have a summer cottage.

Within six months, we are living contentedly in the hired-man's house on a dairy farm for a rent of $50 a month. Though I've never done carpentry before, I learn quickly. I rebuild the inside of our homely little love nest with the weathered barn board that is the architectural fashion at the time, insulate it against the 40-degree-below-zero nights of the legendary Vermont winter, and deduct the cost of my labors from our already miniscule rent. The farmer fences off a nearby parcel of land with an electric wire barrier to deter his voracious cows so I can plant a vegetable garden. He also allows me to take all the old cow manure my wheelbarrow can carry.

That first summer I grow juicy red tomatoes, sweet corn, cucumbers, squash, lettuce, spinach, carrots, cabbage, scallions, broccoli, and pole beans. Marcia grows a beautiful little garden of herbs and flowers. By mid-August, all is in full ripeness and bloom. The nights are cool, my body is tired in the best way, and I sleep well. My industry and simplicity feel worthy of Thoreau himself. In the evenings, I read my well-worn volume of Robert Frost, and feel that for the very first time in my life, I understand his pithy wisdom that "the fact is the sweetest dream that labor knows."

Proud and delighted with my rapid transformation into a full-fledged modern back-to-the-land pioneer, I invite my father and mother to visit.

"You seem to be taking early retirement," my father observes with some skepticism. But he bites enthusiastically into an ear of my sweet corn, and the rich butter trickles at the corners of his mouth. We are sitting at a table we've set up for lunch in the front dooryard of our little cottage. All the bounty of our gardens is piled high between us. We drink red wine in the warm sunlight and listen to the midday buzz of a million grasshoppers.

"I haven't retired at all. Look how hard I've worked to bring all this to your lunch table."

"You can't buy tomatoes like this in the store anymore," my mother says supportively.

My father drains his glass of wine.

"What are your plans?" he asks.

"What do you mean?"

"I mean, after this."

"This is my plan—for the moment. Beyond this I have no plan right now."

My father pours himself another half-glass of Cabernet.

"Yes, well this is all fine and dandy right now, but it won't be so pretty when you're fifty."

I look at him incredulously. Naïvely, I must have expected that he—the master gardener of my childhood—would be impressed and even delighted with my efforts.

And fifty? That's endlessly far from now!

It feels as if a small cloud has passed in front of the sun and the air in the front yard suddenly cools. Probably I say something defensive, wrapped up as I am then in the self-importance of my creative experiment in living the simple life. And I am still too threatened by his sharp and categorical proclamations about my life, and everyone else's, to be able to put myself in his shoes.

If I had been able to do so, I would've found those shoes to be full of contradictions.

On the one hand, he was a child of the Great Depression, whose own father was almost fatally injured when he was only nine years old—legs crushed when he walked between two seemingly parked cars on a New York street and one of them suddenly moved. His father couldn't work at all for more than a year. The memory of this family misfortune, against the larger backdrop of so many other families struggling just to survive during those years, probably remained with him all his life, as an abiding sense that the world could be harsh and uncertain.

Yet on the other hand, these experiences had not made him acquisitive, or overly obsessed with money. He was, that summer in Vermont, in his mid-fifties, and by his own admission, his finances were hardly healthy, doctor though he might be. Though he had always worked hard, he never put the accumulation of wealth anywhere near the top of his priorities. From childhood on, I heard stories of his treating poor patients for free, of how his medical partner in private practice cheated him out of many thousands of dollars, of how he stood up before his colleagues in the American Medical

Association and shocked them by telling them that they should pay more attention to the welfare of their patients than to that of their pocketbook. After that, many of them branded him a socialist.

"You took the Hippocratic oath," he challenged them, "not the hypocritical one."

In temperament, there had always been much more of the poet in him than the businessman. His large-heartedness was legendary. Shortly after his fiftieth birthday, the year after he helped extricate me from that drug bust in Cape Cod, he attended what he thought would be a political rally, only to discover that the room was filled with the families he had served for the past twenty-two years, more than six hundred people honoring him with a surprise party. The testimonials went on for hours.

Sitting next to him at the head table, I leaned over and whispered to him, "Dad, you're the only man I've ever met who is getting to attend his funeral while he's still alive."

Now, as we sit at the table in the summer grass in Vermont, he softens his tone just a little:

"Oh well, you come by it honestly," he says philosophically. "As they say, the apple doesn't fall far from the tree."

"You mean, being a dreamer?"

"Yes. And even more than your old man, if such a thing is possible."

He drains the cabernet.

"Pass me another piece of corn," he adds heartily. But we eat the rest of our feast in silence.

Old Lindy, the neighboring tenant farmer, dies on the night of the full moon in March.

At first I don't know it's him. I'm driving home up Black Falls Road. The enchanting, silvery light of that fat moon pursues me playfully through the still bare branches of the surrounding woods. How I love this road! I love that it's unpaved. And how it winds its leisurely way up into the soft green hills above the little hamlet in northern Vermont that's been my home for the past four years.

Then I notice another narrower beam of light off to the side and below the road. Obviously someone else has noticed it, too. There are now several other lights. As I near them I see that they belong to a truck parked precariously at the edge of the slope leading down to the stream.

Black Falls Creek is always pretty shallow but in full spate now, carrying the snowmelt down from the Green Mountains. As I stop my car and get out to take a look, I can hear the stream singing.

Two men are climbing up and down the bank. They're locals—one a dairy farmer, the other the owner of the gas station in the village. The farmer points his flashlight at his companion, who is dragging something up and out of the rushing water.

In the sharp, bright beam I can also make out the form of a small tractor, turned over so that its strong wheels seem to seek uselessly for purchase in the velvety night sky. Its headlight is still shining, illuminating the woods on the far bank. This is the light I'd seen first, and no doubt the light with which its driver had seen the last things he ever saw.

"I'll be damned if it isn't Lindy!" cries the farmer as his

companion pulls the waterlogged body out onto the near bank at his feet.

He aims the merciless flashlight beam down on the bluish, drowned face.

"And I had a drink with him only an hour ago."

I think of my first meeting with Lindy, four years earlier. I've been told he has the best eggs at the best price in the area, and it's true. It turns out to be a match made perfectly for this earth.

On one side, a young, overeducated city slicker with energy to burn but no real experience in living off the land, despite his Thoreau-inspired pretensions.

On the other, a poor, alcoholic farmer who calls his laying hens affectionately by name whenever he takes an egg out from under one of them. His tomato plants grow high and strong as Jack's beanstalk, with tomatoes hanging like giant red lamps from them all summer long. And he knows more about making maple syrup than anyone I've ever met, or will ever meet again.

Maple syrup comes to seem to me a substance at least as precious as gold. And just as a prospector must sift through tons of rock, so the syrup farmer must boil entire tanks of maple sap to extract its golden nectar. The rule of thumb among New England farmers is forty gallons of sap to make one gallon of syrup. That's a glass of sap for a teaspoon of syrup, and a teaspoon of sap for a single golden drop of syrup. And so forth. The poetry of it enchants me.

But even better is the reality of it, and I must find a master to teach me about that. Lindy knows all there is to know about maple syrup, but he has no maple trees of his own—only his little plot near Black Falls Creek, where his bountiful garden of corn, beans, and tomatoes are the tallest vegetation.

This proves not to be an insurmountable problem, however. His own tiny plot is surrounded by larger farms with maple trees in abundance, owned by farmers who have not the slightest interest in getting the sweetness out of them.

"Too much work and not enough money in it anymore," says farmer Pete as he bends over once more to pull the udders of one of his hundred cows for the ten thousandth time. "You're crazy to bother." He looks at me scornfully and moves on to the next cow chained in the next stall. First prime the teat, then fasten the vacuum pump. Every dawn and every evening of every day—regular and dependable as the rising and setting of sun and moon—Pete milks those cows. No exemptions even for Christmas or the Fourth of July.

Once when I tell him that Marcia and I are going to New York for the weekend, he looks at me wistfully: "Lucky man. I hope I see it someday," he says. "I haven't had a real vacation in twenty-six years."

Still, perhaps out of nothing more than curiosity, he lets Lindy and me tap his beautiful trees that spring, asking only for payment in kind—a gallon of whatever we make. "If you make anything worth tasting, that is," he adds with a slightly malicious grin. At that moment, the saucy bovine he's milking releases a prodigious greenish-brown lava flow from her rear end. Patiently he squeezes one more jet of sweet creamy milk from another part of her anatomy.

"Good luck!" he grimaces, and reaches for the suction pump once more as I take my leave from his cavernous, odorous barn.

But with Lindy's skill and my drive, it turns out that we don't need luck. March is the month for making maple syrup. It is the month of the beginning of snowmelt; of deep, chocolate mud; of the first tentative little reddish nubbins of bud on the dignified silver-gray maples; of the rising of the first pure sap from the earth up through the majestic trunks of those lovely trees. It is also the month when winter in New England sends out its false promises that it will be over any day now. False because the snow inevitably returns at least a few more times in April, and occasionally even in the beginning of May. It's said that more New Englanders commit suicide in March and April than at any other time because of the false promise of spring.

But if there is a farmer's equivalent for catching a wave, or even for riding that deeper tide in the affairs of men, it lies in tapping the maples just as the first sap is pushing its annual way up against gravity into their high branches. You have two weeks—three at the most in a rarely bountiful season—before the sharp alternation of freezing nights and warm days gives way to a duller, continuous mildness, a complacent weather that turns the sap gradually from a clear crystal to a yellow resembling the color of urine. At that point, the most precious wave of sap is past.

Lindy knows all this, and more. He knows the urgency, and the artistry, of catching this sweet wave at just the right moment. The work is strenuous—placing hundreds of taps in the trees, hauling an equal number of buckets of sap to the tank on the tractor, dumping those tanks of sap into the boiling stove in the sugarhouse, cutting and stacking the wood, feeding the fire, watching the boil with a mindful eye.

He shows me exactly how—and how not—to do everything connected with this art. He shows me how to read the weather and the earth for the first clues to begin the sugaring season on precisely the right day; how to drill the taps into just the right places on the trunk, like a doctor looking for a suitable vein from which to draw blood; how to feed the wood beneath the simmering tank so that just the right level of heat will boil the sap down to just the right consistency; how to keep the fiercely bubbling sap from overflowing the sides of the cauldron with a single well-placed dollop of butter.

Then he puts me to work. Our partnership works because of his mind and my muscles. It's an eminently fair karmic exchange that I never for a moment question. To me it is magic. I love his arcane yet wonderfully useful knowledge of so many earthy things, and his gentle, patient way of imparting it. My interest and appreciation in turn seem to give Lindy's own life new sap and purpose.

*Lindy and I in maple sugaring season, Spring 1972.*
*Photograph by Marcia Shibata.*

What a sweet partnership we have during those first springtimes working together!

I see him now in my mind's eye, standing in his shabby overalls in the doorway of his little cabin by the stream in the bright morning sun, holding up a slender glass of maple syrup to the light:

"Look at this syrup, Frank. It's perfect! It's fancier than fancy. You should taste it. Come over here."

He holds the glass out to me like wine. "Oh, I feel like a king this morning, Frank. I feel just like a king!"

The analogy is surprisingly apt, as I soon discover. It turns out he's an Englishman, actually born there. Mr. Lyndon Bolestridge. It seems such a big, formal name for such a little, utterly unpretentious fellow.

Befitting his sense of dignity, he never speaks of himself as a poor farmer, despite the subsistence living he barely ekes out year after year, and whatever else he may think of himself when he's had too much to drink within the lonely confines of his little cabin. Instead he speaks of himself as a gentleman farmer, and tenant to no other man. He speaks proudly of owning his own land, and of having all he needs on that plot of ground.

"Here Sookie, you try some, too," he adds, extending a maple-coated finger down to the eager waiting lips of his portly little mongrel dog—the surrogate wife who sleeps on his bed with him each night, especially in winter when the thermometer outside his windowsill reads forty below. She licks it off greedily and he gives her yet another.

The first year we do it all Lindy's way from beginning to end—selling the syrup in bulk to the local wholesale distributor. We fill nearly a dozen nine-gallon metal milk cans, each with its own grade of syrup, depending upon when in the season it's been made. The higher the grade, the better the price. Lindy is delighted. For my part, it provides enough income to take me well into the summer on my frugal budget. For the first and perhaps the only time in my life, I can truly say I'm living on the land and off the land at the same time. The reality of this makes me happy in a deep, quiet way.

The following spring, I share a brave new idea with Lindy. We could put the precious stuff in pint cans with rustic silk-screened labels that Marcia will design, and sell it directly to retail stores.

"We'll call it Black Falls Farm Pure Maple Syrup and peddle it to Zabar's deli in New York. They'll love it there."

"What the hell is Zabar's?" Lindy asks through narrowing eyes. For Lindy, New York might just as well be the Land of Oz. He is dubious about letting any of the golden liquid out of his sight before he gets the money for it, and tells me so, more than once. But when I reassure him that I will do all the work of canning, transporting, and selling my half, we compromise, agreeing to unload half the second year's crop the old way in Lindy's dooryard and the rest in far-away New York, and to split all the proceeds equally.

When I return from our Emerald City with three times more cash than Lindy has pocketed the week before, and hand him his half share, he needs no further persuading. The next spring, we sell it all in New York.

The rest unfolds like a biblical parable, like a tragic little drama.

When I return from New York that following April, flush with cash, Lindy is strangely silent. When I proudly hand him well over a thousand dollars, he isn't grateful, but bitterly suspicious. He accuses me of stealing from him by withholding some of what is rightfully his. He simply cannot believe that any partner would treat him honestly when so much money is at stake, and that I must be keeping more for myself.

I'm stunned, and stung. I tell Lindy that it breaks my heart that he doesn't trust me after all the great work we've done together. I tell him that what I've learned from him is worth much more to me than money could ever be. I tell him that if he needs it, I'm happy to give him more than half, and that he can have part of my share.

He looks at me as if I've taken leave of my senses. There is clearly no further possibility of persuading him. He takes his share without another word and shuts his door. We will not work together again, and rarely even talk to each other after that day. I feel the sadness of it, but move on. The next spring I sugar again for the last time—alone.

I rebuild a collapsing old sugar shack in the woods and scale down my operation to the small grove of trees surrounding it. There's a lot less money this time, but I've learned well from Lindy: the syrup is sublime, and I raise a little toast of gratitude to him in the solitude of my sugarhouse.

On the last day of that sugaring season, Lindy drives home drunk on his tractor and drowns in Black Falls Creek in the light of the full March moon.

# Part Two: Falling in Love with a Buddha

# Chapter 7

When you think back on first meeting someone—your mate, your lover, or your best friend, for example—you can remember it as a particular time and place, a particular situation with its unique details. It was *the* first time, and every experience you have with that person afterward is not.

With Rinpoche it was different. Meeting him, no matter how many times, was *always* the first time. For that matter it was always the last time as well.

I actually met him for the *very* first time in Lindy's sugarhouse one spring day, by proxy, as it were. I still hadn't seen him and didn't yet know what he looked like. But I'd come upon just a few words of his in *Meditation in Action*, a little saffron-colored book with a beautiful red Sanskrit letter on its cover, and from that day on he was with me as though we'd always known each other:

> Buddha never claimed that he was an Incarnation of God, or any kind of Divine Being. He was just a simple human being who had gone through certain things and had achieved the awakened state of mind. It is possible, partially possible at least, for any of us to have such an experience.

"Yes, of course," I would tell myself happily as the maple sap bubbled nearby. "Somehow I've always known this. I was just waiting for someone to put it into exactly the right words."

*Chögyam Trungpa Rinpoche at Tail of the Tiger (later Karmê Chöling), circa 1971. Photograph by David Lewiston.*

Fifteen months later, on an afternoon in early June of 1974, as I sit in a high school auditorium in Boulder, Colorado, in a crowd of perhaps five hundred young spiritual seekers like myself, I see a short Tibetan man in a lightweight three-piece suit make his way to the stage with a noticeable limp. He is clean-shaven and attended by a young American man my age, also clean-shaven and dressed in jacket and tie. His jet-black hair is long but neatly groomed.

This cannot possibly—I say to myself—be the teacher I've just driven two thousand miles to meet! Can it?

Half an hour later, I've just learned to meditate in the Buddhist way from the simple instruction he gives to the whole lot of us. He sits with uncanny stillness up on the drab stage as he speaks to us, occasionally sipping something from a ceramic goblet on the side table by his chair. Behind him a fading banner celebrates the local football team's exploits from ten years before.

"It's very simple, actually. Follow your breath. Go out with your breath. *Be* the outbreath. Tschoooo!"

He proclaims all this in an unforgettably high-pitched voice with a distinct British accent, emphasizing it with an exuberant gesture of his right arm sweeping out into the space onto the tops of our heads like a strange blessing. His sudden smile is dazzling. Then it vanishes without a trace back into his stillness.

We all sit and meditate together. My mind wanders idly to this thought and that. Meditation is boring. I just want to look at him right now. Is that allowed?

*Come back to the breath!* I chastise myself.

I sneak another look. He's still immovably there. I notice that his left arm hangs somewhat lifelessly at his side.

"Why do we follow the outbreath?" a student asks him afterward. "Why not the inbreath?"

"Well, it's like coming home from a hard day at work," Rinpoche begins, reaching for the goblet and taking a long swallow. "When you go to the kitchen, open your refrigerator, take out a beer, go to your TV room, turn the TV on, and flop down on the couch, the next thing you do is *never*—"

Just then he makes an exaggerated sucking sound on the intake of his breath. It seems to almost drain the hall of air, and to compel all of us to hold our breath for a moment, too. Then the whole audience's energy releases in a wave of laughter. As if he has just delivered a perfectly timed punch line in a transcendental comedy club: Of course! The outbreath! Got it! Laughter itself is an outbreath. Never noticed that before.

"It seems to be connected with some sense of *relaxation*, don't you think?" he adds with a wide grin as the hubbub subsides, taking another draft from that clunky goblet. I look around at the smiling faces of bearded men and beaded women.

*Who is this person?* I ask myself. I resolve then and there that I must find out more.

And it seems that with every step I take to find out more, or to meet him again, a peculiar cosmic law is operating. It dictates that my life will fall apart a little bit more.

Before I leave Boulder that summer, after only six weeks of studying with him, Marcia and I are already going our separate ways after five years of what had previously seemed to be a very happy marriage. Each of us has a dalliance with someone else in the experimental, almost circus-like atmosphere of the new college Rinpoche has created—she with her handsome sensory awareness instructor, I with an adventurous young woman who likes to hike with me in the Rockies among the wildflowers above the timberline.

Somehow Marcia and I return to Vermont in the same car, hoping against hope that we might put our relationship back together after wounding each other so wantonly. But it's too late, and one balmy summer evening we pass the point of no return.

We're camping near an idyllic pond somewhere in Kansas. The sun is peacefully setting and a jewel-like crescent moon is rising on the opposite side of the vast, clear sky. The wind moves gently through the high green prairie grass. Perhaps a hundred yards away a man fishes in silence, smoking his pipe. Now and then a little red glow peeps from the bowl, and then fades out, like the light of a firefly.

We stand by the still water, arguing. At first the timeless serenity of the scene makes a restraining impression on both of us, and we wage our warfare in urgent whispers so as not to disturb the fisherman. We go on this way for a while, our self-consciousness and our bitterness contending with each other for the upper hand.

But at last Marcia decides that words are inadequate to express her true feelings. She pulls her wedding ring from her finger and with a swift, forceful gesture, throws it into the middle of the pond. It plops like a stone and sinks into the reddish-gold water.

Our marriage is over. The rest—though it will take nearly two years—will just be working out the details.

Three months later, I meet Rinpoche again. I leave the hired man's house on the Vermont farm where Marcia and I have spent the years of our marriage together, and move to his Tibetan Buddhist retreat center, only sixty miles away. It is odd, humorous even in a painful sort of way, to discover that I had journeyed two thousand miles to meet him, when he's already been teaching regularly for several years on a piece of land barely more than an hour's drive from my

Vermont home. I feel as if my life is becoming a trick he's playing on me at every turn.

Arriving there on an Indian summer evening in September, I feel like a refugee from my former life. I feel great sadness over what I've had for the past five years with Marcia and now have no longer, and even greater anxiety over leaping into a new world and a new phase of my life with such a sense of nakedness, such utter uncertainty.

I have no real plan beyond the longing to go where I know I will find him again, despite the havoc his presence seems already to be playing with my life. I am nearly twenty-nine years old, but in my guts I'm riding the shakiness and turbulence of a kind of second adolescence. There is no way to hide from the reality that I'm starting over.

To compound my sense of desolation, the residents of the center don't provide me with a soft landing. Not in the slightest. Though they're not really unkind, they're certainly not friendly, either. I arrive at twilight, driving my car—packed to the roof with all my worldly goods—up to the door of the main farmhouse.

Seeing a few men my age sitting on the front porch in the warm Indian summer evening, I smile in greeting. They douse my smile with expressionless gazes. No one stands up to greet me. No one offers to help me unpack or even to point me in the direction of an officially welcoming face.

I soon realize that I should not take any of this too personally. After being there a week, I notice that every newcomer is treated in this cool, distant manner. I wonder at this. What are these people trying to communicate with their refusal to extend warmth in the expected, familiar ways? I get a powerful and at least a partial answer within the month, when Rinpoche arrives to teach a seminar. During one of his talks, he says:

"We are alone, completely alone, by ourselves. Nobody is really, fundamentally, going to comfort us at all. For that matter, nobody is really going to show us the path."

He continues, speaking as if to each of my innermost hopes and fears:

"All of this is very frightening. And you cannot blame that situation on anyone: you can't blame it on the teacher who led you to it, and you can't blame it on yourself, that you started on it. Blaming doesn't help. Going along on the path is the only way to do it."

He gives the unmistakable message that practicing meditation in an authentic way will not be easy, and that there are absolutely no guarantees. Nevertheless, buried in his uncompromising presentation, there is always a note of genuine encouragement, which he delivers directly from the heart just when you are about to give up hope altogether:

"Making friends with ourselves is not very easy. It is a very profound thing. At the same time, we could do it. We could make it!"

The seminar lasts a week. As Rinpoche goes further and further with his teachings about the need to walk on the spiritual path without expecting help or salvation from outside, my loneliness deepens:

"Nevertheless, involvement with ourselves means making an honest relationship with ourselves, looking into ourselves as what we are and realizing that external comfort will be temporary, that our comforters may not be there all the time. There is the possibility of us being alone. Therefore there is more reason to work and go along with the practices that are involved."

Students who have been living here longer than me seem to gain daily access to him during his seasonal visits in ways that I do not. It seems to me that, yes, perhaps the path is lonely, but for some it is apparently less lonely than for others. Entertaining all kinds of fantasies about what the others must be experiencing while they hang out with him, I begin to feel quite sorry for myself.

As time passes, I learn how personally and poignantly Rinpoche is drawing upon his own experience in teaching us as he does. He had been separated from his beloved spiritual master at the age of nineteen, when he was forced to flee Tibet only hours ahead of the pursuing Chinese invaders. They would never see each other again. Later he learned that his guru had died in a Chinese prison.

But then there is still so much I do not know about this strange and compelling person. Much of the time, especially when he is teaching, it is as if he exists only in a timeless realm removed from the ordinary vicissitudes his students might be experiencing. From this realm, it's as if he keeps endlessly delivering messages that can only be described as perfect—unerring in their accuracy and their compassion.

It's clear that he's a human being, especially when he limps into the tent where he gives his talks, leaning on the arm of one of his students. Yet, in another way, he isn't quite human in the way that we are. To this paradox he presents—of being both human and not human at once—no one, least of all himself, ever offers a final answer.

On the last day before his return to Colorado, it is announced that there will be a picnic, and that everyone will have a chance to greet him during the festivities. At first, I'm very excited. This will be my first chance to meet him face to face. But as the day wears on, my excitement gradually gives way to anxiety.

As I consider the situation objectively, it seems quite clear to me that I will have only a moment with him, and that therefore there's actually a great deal at stake! I've learned that he visits the center four times a year to teach—once each season. If this is the case, he will not be back until December or even January.

Then I visualize, as if peering into a dark tunnel, the bitter cold Vermont winter spent with all these chilly people. Can I even hold out that long? Never has the retreat center felt so much to me like a prison as in that moment of self-absorbed calculation.

Finally I find myself standing near the end of a long reception line at the end of a long and somewhat boring picnic. One after another, students have their moment with him. He sits in a simple lawn chair. He drinks now and then from a glass on the wicker side table. As the line inches along, I notice that each encounter seems quite distinct: there is no predictable routine at all. With one student he might nod without speaking; with another he might say a word or two; with still another he might speak at some length and with considerable energy. Occasionally he shakes a hand being offered or returns a hug or even offers a playful kiss to a female student who openly flirts with him.

And just as on that day in the auditorium in Boulder,

there is that uncanny stillness to which he returns after each moment of meeting. It is an abiding openness, into which every italicized instant of interaction flashes vividly, then disappears without a trace.

I do not fully understand the meaning of what I'm seeing. It will take many years of being in his presence, and of contemplating the connection between his teachings and his behavior, for me to begin to grasp even slightly the message of what he's displaying. But over time, I see that whatever he does seems to arise simply and entirely as a response to whatever is coming toward him in that moment, and only that moment. He will play with whatever presents itself to him, and in that moment he is nothing more nor less than that play, that response. And then the presentation ends and he remains: just there. Unchanged. He is simply, utterly there—monumentally there, like a boulder or even a mountain.

Yet terrifyingly *not* there at the same time.

What *is* that and why is that?

It seems to be because he has no nervous little idiosyncrasies, no distracted gestures, no anxious filling of the little gaps in time with small talk or any other habitual tics of behavior, no turning this way and that to find familiarity or refuge in conversation with a nearby crony.

Indeed, as all of us who study long enough with him invariably learn, you can never be his crony or his buddy, no matter how long you may have known him or served him or studied with him. Many will try, but none will succeed. Again and again, in slightly different words each time, he tells us:

"It is only through your commitment to the discipline of

your meditation practice that we have a true connection, or any connection, for that matter. Without that, our connection is doubtful. So please, keep sitting! Maintain your practice."

Many years later, I stand in a crowd awaiting the arrival of one of Rinpoche's own root teachers and spiritual fathers. He is a huge old Tibetan lama whose unusual height, kind yet penetrating eyes, awesome presence, deep, sonorous voice, and capacity to expound the dharma in lucid and poetic language for twenty minutes at a stretch without pausing have earned him the nickname "Mister Universe" from his own closest students and attendants.

As he walks by—supported under each arm by two monks—I hear someone near me whisper in a hushed and reverential tone, yet not without humor, "There goes Space!"

Yes, that's it, I agree with a chuckle of recognition. It is that same indescribable sense of being so fully there, and so utterly not there at the same time, that I've experienced for years so often before with Rinpoche.

"There goes *Space*."

The line keeps shrinking. What will I say to him? Should I ask him an intelligent dharma question? Perhaps I should ask him something about loneliness and the need to walk the spiritual path without leaning too hard on anyone else. I can show him I get his message. Can I possibly impress him in some way? Will he see through that? Of course he will. What can I possibly say? He smiles at the student in front of him. Will he smile at me when it's my turn?

Clouds are gathering and the air is getting cooler. Will it start to rain before I reach him? I ask myself almost hopefully. Will they call the rest of the reception line off? What could I possibly ask him? Probably about being alone. No, too obvious ... and by this time I've worked myself into a frozen inner corner of indecision and panic.

The student in front of me shakes Rinpoche's hand briefly without speaking and goes on his way. I envy the composure and economy with which that person has just handled himself. It is my turn at last.

I approach him. My mind is spinning uncontrollably. He sits unflinchingly still and completely at ease. His only movement is his eyes, which follow me closely as I approach. Now I stand directly in front of him. His head seems massive, almost adamantine. His face is large and round as a full moon. His hair is glossy and very black. A subtle, pleasant fragrance emanates from it.

I prepare to speak—

"Don't try so hard," he says gently before I can get any words out.

My mind stops moving, abruptly. He looks at me with what seems like a trace of curiosity. My senses are suddenly heightened. I notice how exquisitely shapely his ears are, with lobes that bend outward slightly like one of the traditional marks of the body of the Buddha.

"I see what you mean," I reply. I flush, probably.

An interminable moment hangs there between us. Suddenly, I want to say more, but can't quite think of anything specific. At this point, I'm just looking for a way to remain in his presence a little longer, uncomfortable though it feels to me. I furtively glance at his glass. It's definitely beer.

"More," he says then.

"More what?"

"Relax more."

I drop my shoulders slightly and try to stop thinking. He looks into my eyes inscrutably. I hope that he will perhaps reach out and touch me with his hand in a reassuring way. But he just looks at me.

"Okay," he says at last.

Then he nods in a way that communicates without any doubt that our interview has just ended. I smile awkwardly and thank him. I feel quite disoriented as I walk away. I wonder if anyone notices.

I will not see him again for four months.

Between that first meeting with Rinpoche and the next one, I sit.

To call it meditation would probably be an overly exalted description of what I am actually doing. But I do sit. In fact, I do little else.

I've actually dabbled in meditation for several years before coming to the retreat center, but in retrospect I can see that it has been child's play. I practiced Transcendental Meditation for two years while living on Black Falls Road in Vermont. Twenty minutes a day, eyes closed, repeating the mantra the instructor gave me and which I'm strictly warned not to share with anyone else. I repeat the mantra again and again to myself until I "transcend." As far as I can tell, this means that I fall asleep.

But it's also true that I invariably wake up feeling more refreshed, and the chronic headaches that have afflicted me for years do in fact disappear. Ultimately, I come to think of it as a high-powered nap. A welcome and refreshing escape, but an escape nonetheless, because the deeper sense of dissatisfaction and yearning in my life persist. Surely meditation must be more profound, more real than this! When I read Rinpoche's book about meditation for the first time, I'm convinced of it.

Then, by the time I meet Rinpoche in Colorado, I've already actually sat a little. Using the instruction to keep my eyes open and follow the breath, I've meditated for as much as an hour on a few occasions. I'm not aware of it at the time, but in these first encounters with sitting, Buddhist-style, I am merely putting my toe into the deep water of his world for the first time.

The first months at the retreat center in Vermont, however, are a full immersion into that bottomless world. To say it is difficult is a cruel understatement. We sit for a month, twelve hours a day, with breaks only for meals, tea, and a work period. After two weeks, a day off, then two more weeks of the same.

And we do this twice in four months.

The first two weeks of the first month's sitting marathon, I'm plagued by a level of physical discomfort that I've never before experienced. My body, which I've trained to hold, tighten, focus, and push itself through countless athletic competitions from early childhood, rebels at this seemingly endless exercise in not doing. I cannot sit still for even a few minutes without experiencing sharp pain in my legs. The distraction from this pain quickly reaches a level that makes it impossible for my mind to follow my breath. I readjust my posture again and again, extending my left leg every few minutes to relieve the intense ache.

Added to this is the psychological discomfort of seeing that many others are able to sit still for long periods without moving. Somehow I expect the women to be able to do this, but to see the men do it as well is quite disheartening! Since my main motivation in life up to this point has been competitive, I feel that I am losing the race to enlightenment. The irony that you win this race by not moving at all is not entirely lost on me, but I'm too invested in the image of myself as a winner to appreciate the humor. What is wrong with me? Why can't I do this? Everything seems to have become a mean little joke at my expense.

When I'm not in the meditation room, I scheme to make my next session on the cushion more bearable. First I bring extra meditation cushions in and place them under my butt and my knees, so that my crossed legs are slightly raised and my hamstrings less stressed. That strategy affords me a little relief, but my crossed legs now press uncomfortably against each other at the ankles. To relieve this pain, I wear extra socks and also bring several smaller support cushions to place between my offending ankles.

Soon my meditation spot and I have come to resemble a kind of Rube Goldberg contraption, or a Leaning Tower of Pisa. Each new strategy I try just leads to pain somewhere else. I am like the cartoon character who pushes the huge bump on his head down in order to flatten it, but only ends up creating an equally large bump on another part of his body. Is it my imagination, or is the otherwise motionless practitioner sitting across from me silently laughing at me? Either way, the humiliation is ongoing. My pride mocks me even more than my uncooperative flesh and bone.

As the second week of sitting ends, the leaves are falling and the temperature is plummeting. The long Vermont winter is quickly approaching. We plunge into our single day off with a desperate, bacchanalian frenzy. All evening the music plays. Stevie Wonder. Bob Marley. The Eagles. The liquor flows and the lights dim. We dance to haunting lyrics about the desperado, who's getting no younger, driven on by his pain and hunger, his prison in walking through this world all alone. Lyrics of one song after another seem to speak directly to my state of mind and my life at this moment. We pair off, slip away to each other's rooms, couple feverishly. None of it seems to relieve the loneliness, but only to deepen it.

Next morning, I awaken all too early in a hungover haze to the insistent, irritating sound of the bell up and down the halls of the old farmhouse, summoning me again to the cushion.

After the day off, my physical obstacles begin to subside somewhat. My body relaxes more and I require fewer props at my cushion. But the relief from this seemingly merciful change in my fortunes is brief. The physical pain proves to be only a screen, a curtain that, once pulled back, now reveals to me a whole other agonizing terrain of ongoing mental speed, distraction, discursiveness, and uncontrollable fantasy.

My mindfulness of my breathing bobs up and down like a tiny lifeboat in an ocean of emotional turmoil. It seems to disappear for hours at a time, then pop up surprisingly long after I'd forgotten it altogether, or perhaps simply gotten used to the certainty that it had sunk to the bottom for good.

I spend much of each day wandering in memories of the past, whether painful or pleasurable. Eventually all those memories and fantasies become a kind of gray desolate sameness, like the sullen November sky outside the window. Painful or pleasurable, they become less charged, more hollow.

In the final week, tormented by boredom, my compulsively scrounging memory—like a tramp in a Dumpster—spends an entire day on the cushion silently regurgitating every rock-and-roll song I've ever heard.

The second month of sitting is slightly less arduous. Part of it seems to be the season. Winter is fully here and there are many brilliant, cold sunny days with pure blue skies and sparkling snow. The transparent light outside often fills the meditation room and the whole atmosphere seems more cheerful and uplifted. Food seems to taste better. During the midday break, walks in the icy winter air are invigorating and make the afternoon session of sitting more wakeful and slightly more bearable. And too, my body has become somewhat more cooperative, my mind a little less speedy.

It is still extremely boring, but I'm inspired for the first time to contemplate Rinpoche's instruction about the different *kinds* of boredom. There is the hot kind, and then there is what he calls the cool kind.

The hot kind of boredom is well known to me by now. Indeed, it's the kind we're all familiar with. It's like an itch I have to scratch. The itch won't leave me alone. It is a relentless feeling of always wanting to be somewhere else than where I am. Fueled by an underlying tension, which Rinpoche refers to as *existential anxiety*, it runs my life off the cushion. Now, for the first time, I allow myself to sit down and really stay with that feeling instead of moving from activity to activity in order to avoid it. Before this, I could never really see just how completely it has always run my life.

When I sit and meditate, it's like I'm an automobile endlessly idling in the garage. The motor is running but I'm not going anywhere. I realize vividly how much of my mental energy is being wasted every day by worry, by stale and repetitive hopes and fears, by over-planning the future and rehashing the past. Yet the engine keeps humming, and most of the time I cannot find the key to turn off the ignition.

The cool kind of boredom first appears when I begin to wear out the energy of the hot boredom. It happens in different ways. One day on the cushion, it occurs to me that I alone am the one creating this constant hamster wheel of desire and dissatisfaction, of expectation and disappointment that churns endlessly on in my head, and that absolutely no one else in this world is doing this to me. And the temperature of the boredom drops.

Or over the course of a day's long sessions, I gradually begin to unhook myself from my addiction to all this mental momentum. Or, alternatively, a sudden sense of openness occurs when my previous fantasy has just collapsed and another has not yet popped up out of nowhere to take its place. For a moment I stop struggling. For a moment I see the beauty of the light in the room. For a moment, too, I notice that others are sitting with me—with all their *own* struggles and challenges. And that they have been sitting with me all along!

The cool boredom begins to infiltrate my meditation when I find myself content—even for an instant—simply to be where I am, right here, sitting in this room with the others who are practicing meditation, feeling my breathing and letting my thoughts and fantasies come and go without chasing them endlessly to wherever they want to take me. Who would ever have thought that boredom could be a minor spiritual accomplishment? I marvel at my teacher's insight, not to mention his sense of humor.

Then one day the second meditation marathon ends at last, and word soon spreads that Rinpoche will be visiting again any day now. I feel a mixture of pride and excitement. It is as if I am a young warrior, eager to show my chief the wounds I have bravely received in battle, and hopeful of receiving military honors from him in return.

Once again he is directly in front of me. This time, instead of standing, I am sitting on a meditation cushion while he sits in a chair. His big, round face seems to hover slightly above my own. He wears red suspenders and a red checked flannel shirt open at the neck, and smokes a cigarette as he looks at me in silence. We are alone in his room. I have never been completely alone with him before. And whatever I have imagined will happen this time feels as if it got derailed even before I entered that room.

Ambitious and accustomed to getting what I set my intentions on, I've learned that the path to becoming one of his advanced students is a three-month seminary of intensive study and meditation practice under his personal guidance. Though I've now practiced long enough to know that meditation isn't especially fun, I feel as if I've gone through a genuine rite of passage, an initiation of suffering and newly gained knowledge. I'm at least no longer afraid of sitting.

I also know that I'm a very good student, and I'm learning the concepts and categories of the traditional Buddhist teachings quickly and easily. Obviously, Rinpoche will be able to see all this, and he will look upon my request to go to the next seminary as a completely reasonable one.

What I haven't counted on in all this is Eve.

For the past few months we've been hanging out together almost every evening. Our sexual connection is enjoyable and our relationship has become a comforting buffer against the boredom and groundlessness of my life during the meditation marathons at the retreat center. For the first time since my wife and I separated, I seem to have cobbled together the semblance of a little domestic world once again. Eve has already attended seminary, and it's through her that I learn that this must be my next move, and that I must get Rinpoche's permission to go.

No sooner has Rinpoche arrived than Eve informs me he's invited her to "spend time" with him. She leaves late one afternoon and doesn't return till the following morning. Next day she leaves again. I remain behind—confused, resentful, jealous, and lonely. I remind myself that I have absolutely no cause for getting so territorial about the whole thing, but my rational mind and my emotions can't seem to agree. When Eve returns to be with me again, she is even more sweet and affectionate than usual, yet instead of enjoying this I turn it into a cause for further unhappiness.

I can't figure out whether I'm more jealous of her being with him instead of me, or of him being with her instead of me. No matter how I consider the situation, the "me" part keeps getting in the way, like a stubbed toe. Absurdly, I even find myself asking, "Whose side is she on, anyway?"

Eve rightfully tells me I'm being childish, and that perhaps we should stop hanging out for a while. This particular dharma teaching—a penetratingly real and personal one—seems to mock all the facile learning I've gained through my books, and even to throw into question whatever realization I might have gained from all that sitting.

As I enter Rinpoche's room for my long-awaited private interview, my inner turmoil reaches a crescendo. I know I can't let my resentment show, or he will surely conclude that I'm not seasoned enough to go to his seminary. At the same time, I don't know how to hide it altogether.

I sit in front of him, frozen in my silence. He does absolutely nothing to help me with my discomfort. His own silence merely heightens it. He takes a drag on his cigarette and places it on the lip of a black plastic ashtray. He looks at me for a long time without saying a word. His dark brown eyes are unutterably gentle and deep. I cannot hold his gaze for more than a few moments before I feel a kind of vertigo, as if I will fall into those eyes and never find a way back out. He seems to wait for me, but without waiting—as if we had all the time in the world.

I try to remember why I'm there and what I came for.

"What's up?" he says at last, taking another drag on that cigarette. It feels as if he's been smoking it for hours.

"I have a request," I manage to squeeze out at last.

"Sure," he responds in a way that is both intimate and noncommittal.

"I'd like to go to the next seminary."

He takes another sensual drag on that cigarette. The space

seems to become solid. The smoke, my words, his slow and deliberate gestures, all encased in a kind of psychological amber. My body, on the other hand, begins to feel slightly hollow.

"What's the rush?" He lets the slightest trace of a smile waft in my direction.

I mobilize in spite of my growing feeling of shakiness and insubstantiality. "Well, I think I'm ready. I just sat for two months, and I've been studying the transcripts from the two previous seminaries, and I feel like I have a pretty good grasp of the teachings you've given in those."

"Uh-huh," he murmurs. He looks at me closely without saying anything further. I realize there's nothing more I can say at this point without being redundant and pushy. I stare at his red suspenders and wait for the verdict.

"I don't think you're quite ready yet," he says gently.

"I was afraid you'd say that."

"Why?"

"Because I want to go so much, I guess."

"That's not a problem, actually. But you have to marinate more."

"Marinate more?"

"Yes."

"I see." I don't really, but I know that he does, and decide to leave it at that for now.

"You should talk to someone about taking the refuge vows when I give them this time."

"All right." My disappointment is almost unbearable. I stare now at the black lacquered legs of his chair.

"Maybe you could talk to Eve about what that is," he adds.

So he knows. Of course he knows! The mention of her

name is like a sudden paper cut on my skin. In spite of this, I feel that now, more than ever, I must summon the courage to look at him. My eyes are moist. I look into his dark eyes.

"Everything is going to be fine," he says.

He leans forward now and puts his right arm gently around my neck. He kisses me tenderly on the cheek with huge, warm lips. The warmth radiates intensely down through my body. The space becomes soft and luminous. I feel as if I'm going to melt.

"Thank you," I say to him helplessly through a little curtain of tears.

"You're very welcome," he replies, with a dazzling smile.

Following Rinpoche's suggestion in our most recent disappointing encounter, I take refuge with him less than a week later.

At the time, I'm not completely sure I understand the implications of doing this, beyond coming out of the closet as a real Buddhist rather than a spiritual dabbler. Even that motivation I regard at the time as a kind of credential—that after years of exploring what's out there, I've chosen the best spiritual club in town. That being a Buddhist is intelligent, hip, cutting edge. All of this appeals to my deeply ingrained intellectual arrogance.

But mainly I do it because it seems to be the next step in becoming one of his advanced students, the next step in getting to his seminary. My mentality is still that of the business deal: if he wants me to take refuge and if it will eventually lead him to accept me into the elite group of senior students, then of course I will do it. Where do I sign?

Over time, I begin to realize that my view is utterly confused. I begin to dimly understand that the promptings I receive every time I'm in his presence are really commands. At times they are gentle, at times they are fierce, but always they are accurate. They are commands because they invariably have the quality of giving me—not what I want, but what I need. This is simply because they are always delivered from a perspective that sees me as I am and not as I imagine myself to be. They are delivered from a place that is free of bias or wishful thinking, a place that cannot be conned by my little games. They are delivered from the clear sky of a Buddha's view of reality.

From the point of view of my pride, which is almost monolithic when I first meet Rinpoche, to speak of following someone else's command—unless that person were obviously in a position to harm me if I didn't—would seem ludicrous. The very word, *command*, smacks of intimidation and unjust authority, of military repression, of National Guardsmen standing like stone in front of the Pentagon in the summer of 1968 while I and my righteous, free-flowing friends put flowers in the barrels of their guns.

But from the point of view of the basic sanity that Rinpoche is patiently training me to embody in my life, all of his commands are skillful and compassionate gifts. Like water on stone, they wear down my stubborn pride, drop by drop, and point me patiently and unerringly in the direction of being a genuine person.

His talk at the refuge ceremony begins on a gentle and reassuring note, but quickly turns somewhat frightening. Traditionally, he says, we look for refuge in the sense of seeking shelter, like coming in out of the storm. We take refuge in the Buddha as an example of someone who really attained enlightenment, in the dharma as the teaching or path he gave for us to attain the same understanding ourselves, and in the sangha as the community of practitioners who follow the path side by side with us, so that we give each other support and encouragement.

So far, so good, I reflect. Clear, neat, even comfortable. Like a perfectly designed machine that has stood the test of time and will take us smoothly to our destination if we just follow the instruction manual.

But then, what did he just say?

Actually, the main point about refuge is that we are now refugees, that we have no homeland anymore. We are all hanging out in no-man's-land. And though we're hanging out together in our little refugee camp, we are each very alone, and we must each make this journey ourselves. We take refuge in the Buddha as our own courage and intelligence, in the dharma as our life just as it is without any ironclad guarantees of a happy ending, and in the sangha as a bunch of refugees like us, a collection of odd men out who have somehow found ourselves together on this path. We cannot lean on anyone else too much as we follow the path, or both of us will fall down.

"You are all odd men out together, it seems," he concludes with a grin. "I'm afraid that is the case."

As if this were not deflating enough, he then gives me my refuge name.

This, I've been told in advance, is his message to each student about the basic spiritual qualities he sees in you, and that you will work with as you develop along your path. The name, I've also been warned by several who have already taken the vow, is simultaneously an encouragement and an insult. Encouragement in the sense that it points to your enlightened potential; insult in the sense that it highlights your neurotic obstacles.

"Wrathless Generosity," he intones clearly as I walk up in a long line of students to receive my refuge name. He presents me with his own calligraphy of my name in Tibetan, with the English translation written underneath. He has adorned the rich black lettering of each calligraphy with his vivid red personal seal.

*Wrathless.* What does that word even mean? Is he saying I'm too angry? Is he saying I'm not? Is he saying I'm angry now but I won't be someday? Is this the neurotic part of me, or the enlightened part?

*Generosity.* Is he saying I'm generous? Is he saying I'm stingy? Is he saying I'm stingy now but I could be generous someday? Is this the enlightened part of me, or is it the neurotic part?

It's as if I am trying to solve a math problem. Then I think of my last interview with him, and of how I sat edgily on a meditation cushion in front of him while he smoked the cigarette and looked at me as if he had all the time in the world. I was tense and uptight and I wanted something from him and he didn't give it to me …

Of course! He sees that I was there to take, not to give. He sees my resentment at not getting what I want. He sees the spoiled child, barely able to contain his urge to throw a tantrum. He sees everything.

And now it's as if he's announced it to everyone else.

*"You're not ready yet."*

Of course I'm not!

The whole thing is intolerable. What am I doing here? This is all a big mistake. What was I thinking when I moved here? Why couldn't Marcia and I work things out? Maybe I should call her tomorrow. We have a day off soon and I could …

*"Welcome to the Buddha's world!"*

His voice, playful and delighted, cuts through my tormented reverie.

"It is so brave to take such a step, ladies and gentlemen. This world has hardly ever heard of such a thing, yet it can be done, and you are doing it! The Buddha is so pleased that you are willing to make friends with yourselves completely. It is like the sow's ear becoming a silk purse, but even better. The sow's ear is already a silk purse. Jolly good show!"

# Chapter 8

"His Holiness wants you to know," says the handsome young Tibetan translator, "that your son is in the dharma."

It is Christmas, and my parents have come to visit me for the first time in the Buddhist retreat center where I've been living now for the past fifteen months without Marcia. She is beloved of both of them, and the fact of our separation has alarmed and saddened them. But they are not here to bring up painful subjects, only to see how their son is doing and to confirm that all is, relatively speaking, well.

I have not told them this, but I have found it such a relief not to have to celebrate Christmas anymore, but to practice meditation on that day instead. Almost as if they already know this, they've traveled to see me in my native habitat, as it were, rather than waiting for me to make the time-honored journey to theirs at this time of year. I'm touched by this generosity on their part, and feel a growing tenderness for them both.

None of these background concerns apply at this moment, however. We are all experiencing the gentle and irresistible power of the force field of His Holiness the 16th Karmapa, the head of the thousand-year-old Karma Kagyu lineage of Tibetan Buddhism, whom Rinpoche, as another high-ranking teacher in that lineage, is hosting in America as his personal guest.

The translator looks directly at my mother, holding her attention no doubt as much with his striking good looks as with the content of his message. My mother looks proud and pleased, but a little confused, as though not quite sure what she should be so proud and pleased about.

*His Holiness the 16th Gyalwa Karmapa. Photograph taken of an image on the wall in a hermit's retreat at the caves of Drak Yerpa, above Lhasa, Tibet by the author.*

My father, for his part, is not looking at the charming young messenger at all at this point, but only at His Holiness. If he is seeing anything like what I am seeing, it is the form of a middle-aged Tibetan man with red- and saffron-colored monk's robes, a high forehead and short-cropped hair, a glorious smile that radiates out from his eyes across the soft landscape of his whole face, and an irrepressibly exuberant, childlike energy that makes him seem almost to bounce out of his chair when he is speaking.

His Holiness listens knowingly and approvingly as his translator tells us in English what he himself has just said in Tibetan. It occurs to me almost immediately that he speaks no English, but also that what he knows as his translator speaks is definitely not dependent on the words. He beams continuously with unfeigned delight.

He begins speaking again. Now he is pounding the top of my head repeatedly and laughing out loud. The sensation is not at all painful, but rather quite invigorating. I feel a sudden jolt of gentle energy.

The translator waits patiently for his master to conclude, then begins to decode for us once more. His Holiness's expression is now slightly more subdued. It feels almost like a shift in the weather in springtime—from full sunlight to a light rain, but all of it an equally welcome blessing for the flowers.

"His Holiness says that whether or not either of you ever practice the dharma in this lifetime, the fact that your son is in the dharma will bring both of you great benefit. There is no doubt about this."

His Holiness places his right hand on my hand and pats it gently. The warmth of it makes me want to laugh and cry at the same time. My father keeps looking at him in attentive silence. My mother keeps looking back and forth between His Holiness and the translator, her confusion permeated with a gratitude she would probably be at a loss to give words to should someone ask her. She feels this last utterance is very significant, and she asks the translator to thank His Holiness.

Now his eyes seem slightly closed, his whole being focused on something else that only he is seeing. He does not acknowledge my mother directly and says no more, but his presence now seems to embrace us all. The translator nods, smiles, and bows gracefully in our direction. Moments later, we take our leave.

"Gee, Frank, he's really quite a guy!" My father speaks first.

"That smile!" my mother says at almost the same moment. Since she is more easily impressed in such situations, I turn with genuine interest and surprise toward my father.

"Did you think so? What was it about him that made you feel that?"

"That smile," echoes my mother. "And the way he touched you."

My father remains silent for another moment. Then he says, "It's hard to put into words. Let me say this, though, and I hope you won't be offended by my saying it."

"What's that?" I ask.

"Well, I like him better than I like your teacher." He pauses. "That's not to say that I don't like your teacher, because I actually do. But I like this one better."

I'm utterly intrigued at this point. "Why do you suppose that is, Dad?"

He thinks again, looking for the right words. Then he says, "Let me put it this way. Your teacher is kind of like black olives. You have to acquire a taste for black olives. But His

Holiness—is that what he's called, 'His Holiness'?"

Amazingly, he says these "religious" words without a trace of his usual irony or skepticism. I nod.

"Well, His Holiness is just like corn on the cob!"

"With butter!" my mother chimes in with a little laugh. "Don't you think so, Ben?"

I assure my father that I'm not in the least offended, and that I understand exactly what he means.

"What did you think about his saying that my being a Buddhist would be of great benefit to you both?"

"It's a nice sentiment," my father says drily.

"And the part about future lives?"

"You know me, Frank. I see no evidence for that."

A conch sounds outside, followed by the ringing of a gong inside, then a smaller bell, up and down the hallways.

"But he's still quite a guy, and I've never seen anyone like him. You know how I feel about organized religion, even all that 'His Holiness' stuff, like the damned Pope. But he's not that way at all."

"I'm glad you enjoyed meeting him."

"How does it go?" His face assumes the rapt seriousness reserved for his stock of favorite quotations from Shakespeare.

"'There are more things in heaven and earth, Horatio, than are dreamt of in your philosophy.' Always something to learn in this world," he concludes, in a genuinely humble tone.

We walk together to the dining hall. It's time for lunch.

I wake up with a fearful start.

The fire has gone out and the cabin is very cold. The

fading rays of the winter sun tinge the wall opposite my spartan wooden bunk. Soon it will be even colder. The orange embers of dying sunlight make me feel so sad and so lonely. But there is no time to dwell on those feelings. I must start the fire again. I get up from my bed, put on a heavy wool sweater, crumple some newspaper, throw sticks of kindling in on top of it, and light the wood stove.

It is the fourth day of my first solitary retreat. Though I have already sat two month-long group retreats, and though I will only be in this tiny one-room cabin for one more night and day before I return to the retreat center, half a mile down the hill, these four days have been even more challenging and difficult than the previous sixty days were.

For one thing, there is no one else sitting in the room with me, to encourage me either through comradeship or peer pressure to keep practicing. Though I have been advised to make a strict daily schedule and stick to it, and though I've done my best to follow that key instruction, there is no one but myself to see that I follow it at all times. For another, there is no one but me to keep the fire going in the February chill. And there is no one but me to cook my meals, and I am not a good cook.

Again and again I find ways to jump off the arduous sharp point of continuous practice.

I read the dharma books I've brought with me, knowing even as I do that all of them are telling me the same thing again and again—sit, sit, and sit some more if you ever want to really understand what all these words mean.

I even stop to read the boring columns from the old newspapers I'm using for kindling before I throw them in the stove.

I masturbate to increasingly elaborate fantasies of women at the center—both real partners and imagined ones. But up here, all of them are imagined. I am totally alone. There is no consummation. Indulging my sexual fantasy is a momentary release of tension, nothing more.

I take a nap every afternoon, making a deal with myself that it will only be an hour, then I will get up, make tea, and resume sitting once more. But an hour becomes two hours, and the fire goes out and the sun goes down and the cabin gets very cold.

I stand at the wood stove as it begins to heat up. I think of Thoreau. Someone at the center told me he read that Thoreau used to go back to his family home in Concord every few weeks during those two years he was living on Walden Pond to get his mother to do his laundry, and maybe to help himself to a few of her fresh-baked cookies. Then back to the cabin!

The thought of it now makes me laugh out loud. If the story is really true—what a relief! Time to let go of yet another heroic role model with feet of clay. I wonder if he ever actually tried to do what I'm now trying to do—meditate alone for ten hours a day in his cabin. I wonder if he copped out and read the Bhagavad Gita for the tenth time instead, or jerked off in his bunk, or took yet another walk around the pond instead of looking directly at the endless ripples of his own turbulent mind.

Or maybe he was already enlightened. Who knows? Who will ever really know?

The fiery flickers of the rays of the setting sun on the single cabin window catch my eye. I turn to look out toward the woods. Only a few feet from the window, a buck is standing in the deep snow among the bare trees. He is not looking at me, but as I take a single step toward the window to look more closely at him, he raises his head and looks directly into my eyes. He makes not the slightest move to flee. He does not seem afraid. His antlers are magnificent. His brown eyes in that moment are deep and soft and calm and fearless.

I think of Rinpoche ...

*Working as a carpenter on the West residential wing at Tail of the Tiger (later Karmê Chöling), circa 1975. Photographer unknown.*

"Are you sure you want to take this step?" Rinpoche asks me. He has recently arrived at the retreat center for his winter teaching visit.

"Yes."

"You can't go back on it."

"I know."

As he speaks to me now, Rinpoche is sitting in his room at the retreat center, where he is personally interviewing me and every student who has requested permission to take the vow with him tomorrow, one after another.

"If you do, it will eat you up from the inside."

"How so?"

"The medicine turns to poison, instead of the other way around."

"Should I be concerned about that?"

"Everyone who takes such a vow should be concerned about that."

He looks at me gravely. Tomorrow he will be giving the *bodhisattva* vow, and I have requested permission to take it. Nearly a year has passed since I took refuge with him. I have been studying and practicing the dharma every day at the center, and working on the carpentry crew that is building the new meditation hall and residential dorms. I've completed two solitary retreats now, and my confidence in my practice is slowly growing. I feel strong and useful.

The bodhisattva vow is the next step on the path. In retrospect, I can see that it is the key step on the path, and that there is really nothing beyond it. It is a vow to dedicate your life to the benefit of others, rather than your own self-interest.

It is a vow to make your life into an instrument of kindness, compassion, and service to others.

At this moment I have not the slightest inkling of the depth or implications of such a commitment for how the rest of my life will unfold. Fixated still on my ambition to climb what I perceive as the organizational ladder of Rinpoche's world, I see this vow as the logical next step toward attending seminary, which I have been longing to go to ever since I first heard about it more than two years ago.

Rinpoche sits before me now in the radiant, majestic form of a dharma king. He wears a beautiful Tibetan robe of ornamented gold brocade. His skin glows with a golden hue. His hair is black as the glistening fur of a panther. His golden ring is exquisite. It is hard to look at him, like staring directly at the sun. Yet I want nothing else and, as I sit in his presence, know without doubt that I have never wanted anything else, terrifying though he is.

I look into his eyes. They fix me with the uncompromising definiteness of what he has just told me with his words. I feel intense fear, and then I relax.

"I think I understand, sir. As much as I'm able to."

"All right."

I sit there a little longer, though I know our business has just concluded. It has just occurred to me that I won't have another chance like this one.

"Anything else?"

"Well, actually there is."

He gazes steadfastly at me in silence. For a moment I feel like I'm climbing a steep rock face without any ropes.

"The seminary is this fall, and I've already put in my

formal application. But I thought I'd just ask you directly now whether I could go this time."

He continues to look at me without expression.

"We'll see," he says at last.

"All right. Thank you, sir." My heart sinks a little but I smile at him.

"Keep working on the new meditation hall," he says as I get up to leave the room. "It will be very good for all the new students who are coming here. It will help people a lot."

I nod.

"We should get it finished before the snow comes, don't you think?" he adds, peering at me.

Next day I take the bodhisattva vow with Rinpoche. He gives me the bodhisattva name Wrathless Warrior. *Wrathless* twice! I ask my meditation instructor what it means; he tells me it's a synonym for patience.

A month later, my application to seminary is rejected.

My first glimpse of His Holiness Khyentse Rinpoche is at a group audience in his residential quarters at the retreat center, where I now sit in the front row beside the woman who will later become my second wife.

Helen has moved to the retreat center from New York. She has been studying the dharma for six years now, much longer than I. She has already been to seminary, and her knowledge of Tibetan Buddhism certainly far exceeds my own. She has even written a master's thesis on Tibetan medicine, and is an accomplished painter. She is brilliant, artistic, and refined. Within a few months, we are living together.

At this moment, we are gazing at the man whose attendant monks call him "Mr. Universe." Like the 16th Karmapa, he has arrived from India as Rinpoche's personal guest here at the retreat center. We know that he has been a spiritual father to Rinpoche, and that their personal connection with each other is profound.

*His Holiness Dilgo Khyentse Rinpoche. Photograph taken of an image in Shechen Monestary, Kathmandu, Nepal, by the author.*

He is immense, and his presence is utterly overwhelming. Certainly he is by far the biggest Tibetan person I have ever seen. His hands are gigantic yet exquisitely graceful. In one he holds a mala, which he moves bead by bead as he recites a mantra. With the other, he turns the loose pages of his practice text, which rests swaddled in its cloth covering, unwrapped each time he uses it as if it were a precious gift—which it obviously is.

He sits cross-legged on his bed. He is naked to the waist; his legs are covered by a colorful blanket. The skin of his arms and torso is smooth and a warm, rich shade of light brown. His long silver hair is fastened behind his head, in the style of a Native American tribal chief. He is strangely androgynous, with the tender sweetness of a loving grandmother, but at the same time the effortless command of an ancient patriarch.

His gaze is serene and seems to encompass everyone in the room simultaneously, without focusing on anyone in particular. His eyes are soft and kind, and sparkle from amidst a web of upwardly rising lines and wrinkles. He has the majesty of a king of elephants.

The feeling of being in his space is indescribable. For some reason I think of my father's greenhouse. It is as if all of us were seedlings, and his bedroom were the greenhouse, and he himself an ineffable mixture of light, space, and a constant mist of tenderness, soaking every seedling equally with its benevolent, fruitful power.

We have all heard stories about his life, especially about how he went into retreat for nine years at the age of thirteen, and wrote a beautiful poem of gratitude to his mother and father before he did, telling them he would repay their kindness by endeavoring to attain realization for their benefit and the benefit of all beings. Looking at him now, the truth of such a story is utterly beyond argument. If he is not the

Buddha in person, then it is unimaginable to me who else could possibly be. Even our own teacher reveres him in a way we have never witnessed him demonstrate toward any other human being.

Around us, other students ask questions. The translator repeats them to Khyentse Rinpoche in Tibetan. Without looking directly at the questioner or the translator, and as if speaking to the space itself, he answers in a low, resonant mumble, all the while continuing to move the beads of his mala and turn the pages of his text. Sometimes he speaks for several minutes. I wonder how the translator can possibly retain all of that deep, melodious river flow of language, and deliver it in English back to the student who asked the question.

I remember only one exchange from that morning.

"How does one extend compassion to aggression in the environment?" asks one student.

I immediately feel that this person is trying to ask about the topic in a very general, theoretical way in order not to disclose his own experience of it, which is actually quite pointed, personal, and painful. I feel this because I know it's exactly what I would do.

"Begin with the person nearest to you," comes the gentle but pointed reply from Mr. Universe.

"How does one do that?"

"First, you do not respond with aggression even if you feel hurt and that the other person is at fault. That is simply adding fuel to a fire that is already very hot and painful."

The translator pauses for a moment and leans toward Khyentse Rinpoche for clarification. Then he addresses the student again.

"And beyond that, you express gratitude to the person who has harmed you."

"Why gratitude? I don't understand that."

Khyentse Rinpoche listens to the translator, responds, then looks directly at the student while the translator delivers his message.

"You are grateful to them for being your teacher, for showing you where you are still reactive and defensive. You are thankful to them for showing you the work you still need to do in order to become liberated."

The student is silent.

"The more irritating the person, the more grateful you should be to them."

Without any discernible pause or shift, Khyentse Rinpoche continues to move the beads of his mala and turn the pages of his text.

That exchange, though I do not connect it with my own life at the time, will turn out to be both poignant and prophetic for Helen and me. As long as we live in a community at the retreat center, studying and meditating and making our contributions to its expansion, our relationship will be harmonious and very enjoyable.

It is not until we are "kicked out of the nest," and leave the center two years later, that the challenges of making our way as a couple in the world will confront us so forcefully, again and again testing the strength of our bond to its limits, and eventually breaking it.

# Chapter 9

Suddenly aware of the concrete floor on which I'm standing, I notice how cold my feet have become.

I'm perched uncomfortably in the corner of the retreat center's mudroom. Named for the mess and inconvenience that springtime in Vermont invariably brings to every farmhouse, after the snow melts and the runoff mires every dirt road and rural driveway, the room is filled with the winter coats, boots, and snowshoes of every resident in the center.

But it is mid-January, not early April, and the clock on the opposite wall informs me—if my tired, blurred consciousness were not an adequate reminder already—that it is nearly two o'clock in the morning.

Outside the single window the snow is deep and bright in the winter moonlight and the night is very clear. The temperature is below zero. I hear the oil furnace somewhere as it labors steadily to keep the piercing cold at bay.

"Is this Mr. Berliner?"

"Yes."

I begin hopping briskly from one foot to another. Why didn't I put on some slippers before coming down here?

No time, it seemed then.

First there was a knock on my door, waking me from a deep sleep. Then there was word of a phone call for me downstairs, announced by a strangely urgent voice on the other side of the door, with no further details. Roused by the anxious thought of a possible family emergency, I leaped from bed and threw on the trousers from the night before.

Three minutes later, I am standing at the only public telephone on the premises, while the chill slowly ascends my legs under my trousers.

"Just a moment."

There is a gap. The other end of the line is silent.

What is going on here? Perhaps I could quickly slip into those insulated Eddie Bauer boots on the floor a few feet away. They seem to be about my size. I stretch the obstinate, short metal phone cord, then my feet, as far as I can, but cannot quite reach the shoes without leaving the phone to dangle.

"Good morning, Mr. Berliner!"

It's too late. The voice at the other end, high-pitched and playful, is unmistakable.

"Good morning, sir."

"How are you?"

"Very well, sir," I lie.

"That's good. It must be cold there now."

"Yes, it is."

More silence at the other end, then a fumbling sound, some static on the line. Wondering if our connection has been lost, I look longingly over at the nearby boots again. This might be my chance …

"I have a favor to ask of you." The voice returns abruptly out of the static, gentle but oddly piercing.

Too late—again! I hop more vigorously from one foot to the other.

"What can I do for you, sir?"

I feel as if I'm dreaming all this. Rinpoche has never asked me for a favor in the two and a half years that I've been his student, nor did I ever expect that he would. Indeed, what favor could I possibly do for him?

"I would like you to tutor my oldest son."

"Of course."

"He needs some help with his reading and his writing. Spelling. Grammar. Could you do that?"

"I think I could."

"That would be good."

"I'm honored that you would trust me with this, sir."

"He will be coming to the center next summer for two months. You can tutor him during that time."

Is it the lovely deception of the anticipation of the enveloping warmth of summer, even though it's six months away? Is it the feeling of having been asked by him to do something real for the first time? Whatever it is, I forget the chill in my feet for a little while. Perhaps they have simply become numb.

"I look forward to it, sir."

"Excellent."

"Are there any particular books you would like us to work with?"

"It doesn't really matter. Whatever you think is most appropriate."

"All right."

"Thank you, Mr. Berliner. Good night."

"Good night, sir."

I hear the click at the other end of the line. Outside the window, suspended from the eaves of the mud room, a massive icicle gleams in the waxing moonlight.

The boy is scheduled to arrive in early July. I have never met him before. But in the months since his father's request to me, I have learned a little about him.

His name is Ösel, Tibetan for "radiant." He has been in this country for only a short time. Born in the Tibetan refugee community in Dharamsala in 1962, and now fourteen years old, he has been reunited with his father only recently. His childhood has clearly been—by my own pampered American middle-class standards—rugged and rootless, with little opportunity for sustained schooling in any one location. This seems to explain the need for tutoring.

I have given thought to what texts I should use to tutor him, but have not come to a decision with any real confidence. The most persuasive choice to my mind so far is that we use one of his father's books about the dharma. But which one? And is that too close to home, so to speak? Will he rebel like any normal teenager at being subjected to his father's thinking and ideas? I am not sure.

*"It doesn't really matter. Whatever you think is most appropriate."*

When he finally arrives at the retreat center on a very hot summer afternoon, I am embarrassed to admit that I have not yet made up my mind. He is small for his age, slender and shy. He is also graceful and athletic, smooth and handsome, with his father's glossy black hair and intelligent, watchful eyes. I can also sense that—like his father—he is mischievous, though perhaps in a more veiled, quiet way.

He does not speak unless I speak to him first. At times, he reminds me of a wild young deer, at others, of a rural cat—one that is not quite domesticated, and prefers the adventure and unpredictability of barn and fields to the indolent comfort of the farmhouse.

On our first meeting, I am surprised to notice that he has brought a book with him. I can't see the title, but ask him if he has been reading it.

He nods.

"May I see it?"

Silently, but without hesitation or resistance, he hands the book to me.

It's a paperback copy of the *Acts of King Arthur and His Noble Knights*.

"Do you like this book?"

He nods again.

"Maybe we could keep reading it together as part of the tutoring this summer. What do you think?"

"Okay."

It's a little noncommittal, but seems to provide enough of an opening to trust that we can move further in this direction.

"May I take the book this evening and look it over?"

"Sure."

"And we'll start tomorrow morning at eleven. Okay?"

"Okay."

I take the book. He bolts through the open door of our meeting room. Moments later I see him running out past the barn toward the swimming hole beyond the lower meadow.

Beginning the next morning, we spend an hour together each day for the next seven weeks studying John Steinbeck's book about Camelot, page by page. Remembering my time as a teacher in the Brooklyn ghetto—and the magic that arose when I stopped trying to impose my agenda on the lifeforce of those children—I let my pupil's intense interest in the book lead us every step of the way.

We start at the first chapter and proceed step by step through the entire saga of King Arthur and the brave knights and lovely ladies of Camelot. Each evening, Ösel writes an essay on the assigned reading. I tell him to write about whatever he finds most compelling in that particular chapter.

In the morning he reads his essay aloud to me, and we talk about what inspired him. We go over every sentence and every word of his essay, correcting every grammatical error and every spelling mistake.

Then he rewrites the essay so that it is flawless.

Finally, we put the revised essay in a three-ring binder.

"At the end of summer, we'll send this notebook of all your work to your father. Okay?"

He nods without speaking. But he seems pleased.

Day after day, our morning hour together flies quickly past. I am delighted at his progress. Is he? It is difficult to tell. But he does the work, steadily and without resistance, and the pages of flawless essays about the lords and ladies of Camelot pile up like treasure.

One morning, he fails to show up for our meeting. It is

a glorious summer day. I search every room of the retreat center, but he is nowhere to be found. Then it comes to me. I walk the quarter mile out past the community garden down to the swimming hole. He is splashing and paddling with a trio of beautiful teenage girls, who squeal with delight as he dives underwater, tickles them, and resurfaces, the shining water flowing off his body like a seal's.

I call to him. Very reluctantly, he returns to our lesson. I feel old and humorless. I remember his father's autobiographical account of how stern and harsh his own tutor was in Tibet, and how he tried to escape the tedious sessions with him at every opportunity. I feel I have been friendly and patient, yet I wonder if I am that tutor now, a generation later.

In the seventh and final week of the boy's time with me, my parents visit the retreat center for the first time in more than a year.

It is late August. I have learned that Ösel has a keen interest in birds, and raptors in particular. He especially likes falcons, and tells me that he is learning to train them. I tell my father, who brings with him an extra pair of field glasses.

One early morning during that week, my father takes my pupil out into the nearby countryside to look for birds. They walk side by side in the dewy fields near the banks of the Connecticut River, peering into the big cottonwoods with their field glasses, looking for raptors. I walk a short distance behind.

*My father, circa 1973. Photograph by Anna Berliner Kelly.*

It is just dawn, and the sun has not yet risen. The light is misty and pearly grey. My father notices a great horned owl on a high branch, almost entirely hidden by leaves. I marvel once again at the keenness of his powers of observation. How does he see these things? He whispers to Ösel and points toward the branch. They peer at the huge bird through their binoculars with quiet excitement. I stay behind, enjoying their enjoyment.

When we return to the center, my father asks Ösel if he would like to visit his home in Connecticut, three hours away to the south. They can continue to look for birds there, as well. We can all drive there together.

The young bird-watcher seems happy to be invited. We leave the next morning.

After dinner the first evening, my father goes to his bookcase, and takes from it a large volume about birds of prey, filled with beautiful color illustrations of hawks, owls, eagles, ospreys, and falcons.

"Look at these." He hands the book to Ösel.

A strange mixture of joy and loneliness fills me. I silently leave the room as they leaf through that lovely book together.

After seven years of teaching and working with his steadily growing community of American students, Rinpoche begins to let the word filter out into our midst that he will be going into retreat for a year.

There is widespread panic. Many have come to feel that he is as vital to their lives as the air they breathe, and that they can't imagine how they will survive without his constant presence. Some try to talk him out of it. Some are angry. Some begin immediately to strategize how they might go into the retreat with him.

He decides to give a community talk to clarify his intentions. He tells us that we have received enough instruction and teaching to sustain us on our own while he is in retreat. He tells us that he will be keeping in touch with us during this retreat in his own way, even if he is not with us personally. He tells us that he loves us and trusts us.

He tells us, somewhat mysteriously, that he feels he has reached a point in his work here that requires him to reevaluate his vision and direction.

*Chögyam Trungpa Rinpoche, circa 1976. Photograph by Bob Morehouse.*

Most memorably, he tells us that we have begun to regard him as a kind of spiritual Jersey cow, to which we can go endlessly for rich, creamy milk. He tells us that we have become complacent and overly dependent, and that we must begin to trust our own understanding and our own inner resources.

We must do this, he tells us, because he will not always be here. Just as he was separated from his own teachers by the Chinese invasion of Tibet, and had to find a way to grow up on his own without them, we may have to do the same before we expect it. There are no guarantees. Life is fickle and unpredictable. The spiritual path provides no buffer, no insurance against the naked, existential truth of things.

He says, chillingly, that we should regard this retreat as a rehearsal. Then he returns to the image of the Jersey cow:

"I am not your Jersey cow. You will not be able to milk me forever. You must let go of that tit. You must produce your own milk."

After he leaves for retreat, I find myself wondering what he is actually doing. I imagine he is in a tiny hut on a mountainside somewhere, or even in a hospitable cave. Rinpoche has taught us extensively about the great Tibetan saint Milarepa, who spent his entire adult life meditating in caves high in the Himalayas and sang glorious songs about his realization. He has told us about Khyentse Rinpoche's nine-year solitary retreat, starting at the age of thirteen. I think of my own first solitary retreat—that poignant four-day struggle in the little cabin a year ago—and am awed at these stories. Clearly, these are not ordinary people. They are, in fact, unimaginable.

As it turns out, he will spend a full year in a summer cottage in rural Massachusetts, generously donated for the retreat by a successful New York playwright who has become his student. The environment will be simple, but comfortable. He will have a cook, a master of his household, and a steady trickle of visitors.

What is he doing? It seems to have something to do with Shambhala. Rumors seep out that he is inventing a whole new way to teach meditation to Westerners, that he is recreating the mythical ancient kingdom of Shambhala here in the present day, to uplift what he sees as a confused and degraded society worldwide, lost in the superficial seductions of materialism. The memory of my father's description of Shangri-la that day he first handed me the book arises vividly in my mind.

Stories come back of a room in the cottage where Rinpoche goes to design banners, pins, insignia of a royal court, and to write essays on the politics of enlightened monarchy, and the protocols for an actual kingdom.

"Enlightened monarchy." As I reflect on my own study of history, it sounds like a cruel oxymoron. Yet whatever he does, you cannot help but wonder and be curious, intrigued. He is endlessly surprising, unfathomable, indifferent to conventional thinking or opinion. A few months before his retreat ends, I'm invited to visit. I am to arrive late one morning, stay overnight, and leave late the next day.

I am very excited about this, to say the least. I will be able to get my own glimpse of what all the rumors have been describing. And I will also have the opportunity to hand-deliver the finished product of my tutoring work with his oldest son. As it turns out, I do not see Rinpoche at all until breakfast the following morning. Meanwhile, I give the binder of Ösel's essays to the master of his household to pass along to him, since it looks quite likely that I will not have the opportunity to do so myself.

I sit down to breakfast with a group of perhaps four other visitors. The table is simple and rustic, and rich morning sunlight flows into the room from an eastern window looking out upon maple trees in their vivid autumn colors.

Rinpoche sits at the head of the table, wearing a simple white cotton kimono with a pattern of blue interlocking chains on it. His cook and attendant have set the table for his guests, and are busy bringing generous helpings of cereal, eggs, bacon, sausage, toast, pancakes, coffee, tea, and orange juice from kitchen to dining room.

Rinpoche appears to be eating some peculiar-looking meat of some kind—perhaps kidneys or tripe. Rumors abound that he is particularly fond of tripe nowadays. He eats slowly and without visible enthusiasm. He speaks little, occasionally stopping to listen to the conversation around him, but without joining in. At the same time, the atmosphere is quite relaxed and comfortable, and all the visitors converse energetically, without apparent concern that Rinpoche is not responding to their repartee.

Predictably, I'm rather nervous about being in his presence. Not knowing the others at the table very well, I keep to myself and focus on the most comfortable option available to me, which is to eat. The bounty of the offerings is irresistible. I pile my plate high, and almost literally dive in. The breakfast is delicious, and the fullness of it settles and calms me.

For the first time since arriving, I feel at home.

At some point, the cook comes out from the kitchen to see how things are proceeding. He announces that there is plenty of food for second helpings, if anyone would like, and looks slowly around the table.

Rinpoche pays him no attention. The other guests shake their heads, complimenting the cook on the tastiness of the breakfast, and assuring him that they've had enough. The cook looks at me and asks, "How about you, Mr. Berliner?"

Noticing that everyone else has declined, but aware also that there is no shortage of breakfast food still to be had, I nod in the affirmative. At the same time, I try to temper my enthusiasm, equally aware that I am the only guest who is returning to the trough, so to speak.

Almost immediately, the cook returns from the kitchen with my plate, overflowing once again with all the tasty offerings I had just packed away a few minutes earlier.

"More coffee, Mr. B?" the cook asks as he puts my heaping plate in front of me.

I am quietly delighted at the familiarity of his addressing me in this way, especially in Rinpoche's presence.

"Yes," I respond with unconcealed enthusiasm, feeling almost entirely at home now.

The reassuring patter of conversation continues as I address myself for the second time to my eggs, sausage, toast, juice, and coffee. Then one of the other guests turns to Rinpoche and remarks, in a voice that can suddenly be heard above the rest, "Mr. Berliner has quite an appetite, doesn't he, sir?"

Rinpoche looks over in my direction.

"He's a growing boy," he observes drily.

There are a few chuckles, then silence. As I immediately reflect that I am only three weeks shy of my thirty-second birthday, it dawns on me quite forcefully that my teacher's comment has not exactly been a compliment. The sense of being so comfortably at home vanishes in an instant, and I am left again feeling alone and anxious, and with the vaguely unpleasant sensation of my tummy pressing a little too tightly against the belt of my trousers.

A few moments later, Rinpoche addresses me again.

"The tutoring seems to have gone well."

His tone is kind and it feels now as if all that kindness

is for me. My spirits rise a little. I feel the familiar tingling warmth all over my body.

"You had a chance to look at Ösel's essays then, sir?"

"Yes."

"That's wonderful."

"He seems to have a keen interest in kings and queens, knights and ladies."

"He does. Well, that was the book he brought with him, so I just went along with it. It seems to have worked out well."

"Yes. King Arthur and Camelot. Quite appropriate."

"Appropriate?"

"Yes. It's about Shangri-la in the ancient British Isles. Quite delightful, actually! Don't you think so?"

His comment gives me pause for a moment. Had I ever talked to him about my fascination with Shangri-la and *Lost Horizon*? Not that I could recall. How could he know?

Then I remember his telling me that cold night on the phone—when I asked him what books to use—that I should choose whatever I thought was "appropriate."

"Oh yes, I understand what you mean," I add.

He looks at me again, more closely, with a smile:

"You do? That's good. That's excellent!"

And he begins to chuckle, in a way that suggests to me that I haven't a clue what he really means.

# Chapter 10

Waking up one morning the following May in a hotel in New Hampshire, I'm pretty sure I'm about to become enlightened. Never have I felt so alive, yet so peaceful at the same time. Maybe at the end of that acid trip ten years ago, in the early morning? But that was the drug. This is something else. Or is it just the fullness of spring in New England, the warm sun and the trees blossoming everywhere on the grounds of the old hotel?

Or is it Rinpoche?

After all, he's just given the "pointing out" transmission to the whole seminary of three hundred students the evening before. It's the moment we've been waiting for after three interminable months of study and meditation practice, three months of boredom and snow and loneliness and washing everyone else's dirty dishes when it's your turn to do the work rotation in the hotel kitchen.

It's the mythic moment when the spiritual master shows you the true nature of your mind. Whatever that is.

It's probably more a matter of expectation than anything else, I suspect. He really doesn't seem to do much at all when the actual moment finally arrives. His silence is perhaps more heightened than usual, the room more charged with anticipation than usual. Then a sudden sharp snap of his fingers this time, more silence, then his voice in a little gleeful crescendo:

"*That's it!*"

More than a few students say later, "Was that really it? Did I miss it?"

But this morning, the feeling of something huge having shifted inside me is incredibly strong, and utterly undeniable. I can't make it go away even when I try. The light in the room is rich and creamy as the early sun comes through the curtains. The space itself seems heavy with this light, which is more like a transparent liquid than mere light. Outside the window the fluid light seems to extend infinitely in all directions.

Is it the space? Is it my mind? How do I separate the two?

And my mind is so still! When thoughts arise in it, they seem to just dissolve in this creamy atmosphere. I deliberately try to generate some anxious thoughts about the future—certainly there's no end to the possibilities there! I've spent most of these three months on my meditation cushion wondering what I'm going to do next with my life. And often when I awake in the morning, a nameless fear quietly slips in like cold fog.

But nothing like that happens this morning. My fears have no traction at all. I'm filled with a quiet joy, one that seems deeper than any well. Can't I just have this experience forever?

Then I remember a teaching Rinpoche gave only a few days ago about the blessing that can pass from teacher to student: *jinlap* is the Tibetan word for it. He describes the real, psychophysical signs of it, the blissful feeling of being enveloped in a rich, gentle, pervasive atmosphere of wakefulness. It's the feeling of being completely engulfed in that.

"Engolloped," he calls it, combining the two words and inventing a new word on the spot in his inimitable way to the delight of all of us. The teacher's mind is almost an entity, he tells us, filled with positive qualities, which the student can receive fully if there's enough openness. Like pouring melted gold into you.

So this is it! This is the *jinlap*, and I want it to go on forever …

"What do you think I should do next, sir?"

"Your guess is as good as mine."

It is only four hours later, and I am sitting opposite Rinpoche in the drawing room of his suite in the hotel. Seminary is ending soon, and he is dressed casually today. His shirt is soft and open at the throat. As he responds to my hopeful question, he lifts his right hand, draws his shoulders up toward his chin, and makes a comical grimace. I feel suddenly as if I'm talking to an unsympathetic Yiddish grandfather.

His answer feels like a glass of cold water he's just thrown in my face. I try to recreate the warmth of the *jinlap* but can't seem to retrieve it.

"You can't go back to the retreat center, though," he remarks offhandedly for further deflating effect.

"I can't?"

"I don't think so."

Not go back to the retreat center?

He can't really mean that! The retreat center has been my home for nearly four years. Everything I've learned from him so far, it seems to me, I've learned while living there. Over time, after much frustration and disappointment, it feels like I've begun to create a real niche for myself. Starting as a lowly carpenter, working long, hard hours to help build the new residential dorms and then the new meditation hall. Then gaining an administrative position as assistant to the center directors. All the while I've continued to study and sharpen my intellectual understanding of the dharma. In the past year I've even given talks now and then, and gotten feedback from others whom I respect that I'm a good dharma teacher. Not to mention having room and board taken care of. I'm just starting to feel completely at home there at last!

And now I realize, I had hoped he might suggest that I could be the director within another year or so.

"It would probably be good for you to begin to teach somewhere else," he adds.

I feel slightly giddy, but slightly queasy at the same time. On the one hand, he's telling me he wants me to teach the dharma beyond the retreat center—an unexpected vote of confidence. On the other, he's kicking me out of the nest quite unceremoniously.

"You mean out in the 'real world' again?"

"Something like that," he says with a little chuckle, as if slightly amused at the notion of a "real world."

"Did you have someplace particular in mind?"

"Not really. It doesn't matter that much. But you should definitely start teaching more."

"But how will I make a living, sir? Nobody is going to pay me just to teach the dharma out there."

Rinpoche looks at me with more amusement. My discomfort grows.

"Your guess is as good as mine."

He lights a cigarette with his beautiful gold lighter, then places it back down on his side table with a slow, powerful movement, as if that lighter were really the thunderbolt of the Hindu god Indra. Where to go from here with this incredibly disappointing conversation? I grasp at the remaining straw.

"Well, what *is* your guess, sir?"

He puffs the smoke of the cigarette in my general direction.

"Probably you should just follow your coincidences," he says at last.

I realize that to ask him for any more clarification about my future would definitely be an act of aggression. I thank him and am about to get up to leave.

"Don't be too much of a bliss junkie out there in the real world," he says with a grin as I'm rising from my chair. "Watch out for the traffic lights."

I walk despondently to the lunchroom and sit alone, eating in silence.

"How are you?" My friend John sits across from me with a hearty greeting, his plate piled high with food. I'm not really looking forward to any conversation at this moment, but there appears to be no way out. I make some noncommittal comments about how seminary is ending and the transition feels somewhat intense.

"What will you do when you leave?" he asks innocently, driving matters immediately to a painful point.

"Funny you should ask. I was just asking Rinpoche the exact same question."

"What did he say?"

"Not much."

The memory of that exchange feels like an actual weight on my body. John seems to sense that I'm not eager to discuss it further, and turns with somewhat irritating gusto to his lunch. We eat for a while in silence.

"You know, I have an idea," he says.

His tone of confidence is bizarre, as if it were coming from some other planet than the one I live on. Part of me is wondering whether his idea has anything to do with me. I look at him without speaking.

"You look a lot like the guys on the billboards," he continues. "You know, the Marlboro Man. The branding iron, the horse, the sunset, the square jaw, and the cigarette."

"I don't smoke, John."

"Of course you don't. That's not the point. The point is that you look the part. It's all just illusion, anyway. Smoke and mirrors. And there's good money in it. There's really good money! Do you know how much those guys on the billboards make?"

"I have no idea. Probably a lot."

"A hell of a lot. And pretty much all they have to do is stand there."

"And … ?"

"You could do it, too. Why not?"

"How?"

"Well that's the idea I was having. You know, my mother runs a modeling agency in Atlanta."

"I don't want to live in Atlanta."

John looks at me sharply.

"Slow down, man! You don't have to live in Atlanta. What I'm saying is that my mother has a lot of professional experience with that world. I could show her some pictures of you and she could tell us immediately whether you could do it. You wouldn't have to do it in Atlanta, particularly."

"I don't have any pictures, John."

"Don't worry about it. I can take the photographs."

It dawns on me that he is completely serious.

"When?" I ask, somewhat shyly.

"This afternoon, and then again tomorrow if we need to. We'd have to do it now because seminary's over day after tomorrow."

There's no stopping the momentum of his certainty about my immediate future. He seems to cut through my every self-pitying objection like a warm knife through butter. I also realize that he's doing it out of a kind of generous extravagance of brotherly feeling, with absolutely no expectation of anything in return.

In spite of myself, I'm touched and heartened.

"Are you kidding me, John?" I say at last, as much with appreciation as disbelief.

"Not at all. You bring the clothes and I'll bring the camera. You've got some nice suits here, don't you?"

By the time we leave seminary forty-eight hours later, John has shot half a dozen rolls of film. Within two weeks, an envelope arrives in the mail at the retreat center, where I am morosely packing up my life and reluctantly contemplating my next move. In it are all the negatives and the contact sheets of the photos he took. About twenty photos are circled in red. Attached is a note from John:

"My mother circled these and said to tell you to have them enlarged and put them in a portfolio. She said that you can definitely succeed at this if you want to. Easily. Good luck!"

*Modeling for Giorgio Armani in Florence, 1979.*
*Photograph by Aldo Fallai in* L'Uomo.

And so begins my career as a fashion model. Two weeks later Helen and I move to New York. I assemble my portfolio, make an appointment at the best men's modeling agency in the city, and start working within days. The work is easy and the money is thrilling. In the next seven years I will work in New York, Los Angeles, San Francisco, Dallas, Denver, Atlanta, Florence, Milan, Israel, and many other places, riding the almost magical energy of this illusion.

At the same time, I go to the sangha's local meditation center in New York, start making myself useful in whatever ways I can, and soon begin teaching dharma classes. I feel with more than a little pride that I am fulfilling Rinpoche's command to me. Every so often, I reflect back on his playful suggestion that final day at seminary that I should follow my coincidences, and tears of gratitude come to my eyes.

It's 1981, and three years have passed since my reentry into the "real world." I'm in Boulder, working at Rinpoche's invitation as the director of the national office of the Shambhala Training program, which he has created out of the inspiration of his retreat four summers earlier, and which is now being presented in cities throughout the United States as an innovative way to teach Westerners the principles and practice of meditation.

I love my job, which gives me more and more opportunities to teach, not only in Boulder but all over the country, and there's a modest but dependable salary as well.

Best of all, I live less than a mile from Rinpoche, and though there are hundreds of other students here making equally legitimate demands on his time and attention, I have more personal access to him now than I've ever had before, or will ever have again.

I continue to model to help pay all my bills, but the initial high has long since faded. In fact, I am now feeling a growing sense of embarrassment that I work as a model. Posing in front of a camera with the latest men's fashions on my back seems more and more tawdry and superficial. Especially when I'm giving lofty talks on the teachings of basic goodness and sacredness in the Shambhala vision of our life in the world, I feel like an impostor, like a whore in church.

Nor can I shake the infrequent but nagging thought that my father is still waiting for me to do something meaningful with my Yale education, and that strutting around for a living with the latest threads draped over me in the pages of *L'Uomo*—even if they've been designed by Giorgio Armani himself—does not in any way fulfill that weighty expectation.

More painful still, is the realization that at the age of thirty-five I still feel any need to live up to my father's expectations at all. But there it is—like an inconvenient pothole right in the middle of my road.

Idly, I pick up the little tattered paperback edition of *Meditation in Action*, in whose pages I first met Rinpoche, and open it at random:

> What is important is to get beyond the pattern of mental concepts which we have formed. That does not mean that we have to create a new pattern, or try to be particularly unconventional. We do not have to turn everything upside down in our pattern of behavior and in the way we present ourselves to other people. That again would not particularly solve the problem.

As always, and in that uncanny way, he seems to be talking directly to me again. How does he do that? I feel a sense of anticipation bordering on impatience. Yes, I understand my own problem exactly as you state it here, Rinpoche. But what is the solution? I keep reading:

> The only way to solve the problem is by examining it thoroughly ... and go beyond mere opinions and so-called common sense conclusions. One must learn to be a skillful scientist and not accept anything at all. Everything must be seen through one's own microscope, and one has to reach one's own conclusions in one's own way.

After sitting with this for a week or so, I soon realize that it's time for me to go talk to him again about my life. The whole dilemma has come to have just the kind of existential tension that feels worthy of bringing to him.

I feel that I've examined the problem quite thoroughly, and the solution I've come up with seems eminently sensible and even somewhat inspired: I will stop modeling and persuade Rinpoche to get Shambhala Training to raise my salary.

I know that you are probably chuckling now, dear reader. Possibly this may seem like the Buddhist version of the old joke, "If you want to make God laugh, tell him your plans." Unfortunately, I'm quite serious.

The encounter happens very briskly. I meet with him in his office at the Boulder meditation center one weekday afternoon. He is conducting a series of appointments as part of his ordinary workday, and several others are waiting in the anteroom with me. His secretary motions me in, reminding me that I have about fifteen minutes.

Rinpoche sits behind his desk, dressed in a beautiful pearl gray suit. The desk makes him feel quite far away, but I've rehearsed my appeal thoroughly and plunge in straightaway.

"Rinpoche, I wanted to say first of all how much I love my job at Shambhala Training, and how much I appreciate your having the confidence in me that I could handle it."

He looks at me skeptically without speaking. My schmooze has obviously fallen flat. He waits inscrutably for my next move.

"And I would really like to devote all my time to it at this point."

"So?"

The dreaded word! I feel now as if I'm looking at him through the wrong end of a telescope. His body seems to recede before my eyes like the Doppler effect of a distant star.

I raise my voice a little, as if to cover the increased distance between us. My words sound like rattling tin cans:

"Well, there's the modeling. I've been doing it for a while now, but more and more I'm feeling like it goes against what I've learned from you and what I'm out there teaching."

He seems to be carefully studying the exquisite blue diamond pattern on his tie. Then he looks up at me over his glasses with a slight furrowing of his brow.

"Mm-hmm."

"So I thought if I stopped the modeling now, and just committed myself fully to Shambhala Training—"

He looks at me directly through the glasses now: "Can you afford to do that?"

Yes! At last the conversation is heading in the right direction! "Well, I could if Shambhala Training increased my salary a little."

"I see."

At this pregnant juncture, he rings a small silver bell on his desk. In a moment, his secretary appears in the doorway. Rinpoche then asks him with considerable interest whether his next appointment has arrived yet. The secretary nods his head, Rinpoche thanks him, and he closes the office door again.

Again he turns his level gaze upon me. I have a sinking feeling that he doesn't remember what we were just talking about. With the force of a desperate general, I marshal my remaining troops for the final assault:

"So what do you think I should do?"

"Do with what?"

"With the modeling. Do you think I should stop?"

*"No. Do it more!"*

He announces this so emphatically that the energy is like a strong wind blowing me back toward the door. At just this moment, the secretary knocks to signal that my time is up and pokes his head into the office once again.

This time Rinpoche completely ignores him, turning his attention entirely to me with a bewilderingly affectionate expression. I feel as if the noonday sun is now shining directly in my face.

"It's always good to see you, Mr. Berliner. I hear from others that you're doing very good work at the national office. And you look quite smashing, if I may say so!"

"Thank you, sir."

"All right. Good-bye."

He nods gently in farewell. I retreat meekly from the field of engagement.

# Chapter 11

It is six years now since that evening in Boston back in 1975 when my father and mother first saw Rinpoche. True to her vow in the car as we headed home, my mother has begun to meditate. When I fly east from Colorado to see my parents every four months or so, she and I sit together each morning after breakfast, in the big, sunny upstairs room where I stay when I visit them.

Not so my father. He cannot get past the idea that sitting down and apparently doing nothing at all is simply a waste of time. He prefers to stay on the screened porch at the breakfast table, drinking his second cup of coffee and reading the newspaper or watching the many colorful species of birds at the feeder on the garden patio, before driving to the hospital to his desk and his students and his staff.

"Ben, why don't you meditate with us today," my mother supplicates him one morning as he finishes the last swallow of his first cup of coffee. Knowing how resistant—even contemptuous—he usually is about the prospect of sitting, she has not asked him for a long time.

To my astonishment, he agrees to join us. He asks me how to meditate. I give him a simple instruction on sitting with good posture and paying attention to the sensation of his breathing. We all go upstairs. My mother and I sit on our cushions. I bring a chair in for my father. My mother seems delighted and incredulous at the same time. My father is actually going to meditate!

He sits down next to us in his chair. Through the open window of the room we can hear the birds calling raucously to each other from the trees in the backyard.

"How long are we going to do this?" he asks me.

"About ten minutes or so."

I show my father the meditation gong I gave my mother as a gift the last time I visited. He looks at it without reaction or comment.

"I'll time the meditation, Dad. I'll ring this gong to begin, and after ten minutes or so, I'll ring it again to end."

He looks at me dubiously, but nods his agreement.

"You don't have to concern yourself with the time. I'll do that. Just practice the meditation the way I told you."

I ring the gong. The gentle sound rises and then slowly fades into silence, and the three of us settle into the sitting. Outside the birds continue to chatter. Now and then my father shifts his legs, but all in all he seems remarkably free from agitation or restlessness. I can hardly believe it.

About eight minutes pass. Suddenly my father almost leaps from his chair and heads for the door.

"Where are you going, Dad?"

"Time's up," he announces quite forcefully.

"I told you not to worry about the time. I said I'd ring the gong at the end of ten minutes."

"Well, according to my watch it's been ten minutes." And without further ado, he opens the door and heads down the stairs. Neither my mother nor I will ask him to sit with us again.

When Rinpoche is really interested in something, he leans forward in his chair. His face is often impassive and inscrutable, with a quiet sadness in the fathomless depths of his eyes. But now he suddenly becomes highly animated. He smiles with the unfeigned delight of a little child.

"How do you make maple syrup?" he asks. His eyes seem to dance.

My meeting with him about Shambhala Training business has just ended. Somehow the subject of maple syrup has come up in its aftermath, and I have volunteered that I have some expertise in this area—always a slightly tricky matter in dealing with Rinpoche. I explain the process to him as succinctly as I can. I try to streamline the story for fear of boring him. I have learned that when he loses interest in something, it simply disappears from the room no matter how much life you may try to breathe into it.

But he seems quite engaged, even fascinated at certain moments. I feel honored, and like a pump that's been primed, I pour forth.

"You have to boil the sap a long time, right?" he asks.

"Yes."

"It takes a lot to make a little syrup?"

"Yes."

"How much?"

"About forty gallons of sap to make one gallon of syrup."

"Mm-hmm."

He sips from his glass of sake and seems to consider these proportions.

"It's like bodhicitta. Don't you think?" he says at last.

"Sir?"

I strain to follow the sudden leap of his analogy. He looks at me in silence.

*Bodhicitta* is literally "awakened heart." It was said by the Buddha to be the source of all our loving, kind, and compassionate impulses and aspirations. And as Rinpoche often reminds us, even the most ferocious animals have this quality within themselves, as plainly evidenced by their tender and constant devotion to their young until they are strong enough to fend for themselves in the wild.

He also calls it the "soft spot," because it is that place in us that is capable of being touched. It is the vulnerable place that can make us cry at the sight of something beautiful, or something that is painful for someone else, or that can make us fall in love.

"Even if you're a person whose only love in this world is chili peppers, still that is evidence that your soft spot is there and ready to be touched," he will say with a mischievous smile. "Even if it's only the love of chilies that touches you, still you are not completely hopeless after all."

Rinpoche never tires of teaching about bodhicitta. Not only is it the awakened heart, but it is also "the heart of awake." In other words, it is the very essence of what is necessary to become a Buddha, or even to become just a decent human being.

"How is maple syrup like bodhicitta? I'm not sure I understand."

"You tell me. I'm sure you can figure that one out."

On the spot, in that familiar place of tension between wanting to impress and fearing I will fail, like an overly eager schoolboy, I hazard my best guess:

"Because it's so sweet?"

"Bodhicitta isn't always so sweet, actually," he responds drily.

I feel a bit foolish that I've not come up with the answer he seems to be looking for. Earnestly, I regroup and try again.

"Because it's hidden inside other things?"

"Something like that," he replies.

He is silent again for a while. I look at him expectantly.

Then he says, "It's the essence of everything, in some sense. The ego is just its disguise."

At this, I remember the story of the renowned meditation master Tilopa who lived in India a thousand years ago. He was a wild and spontaneous yogi, much like the inconceivable person sitting right here in front of me. It is said that he lived on a beach, ate fish heads, pounded sesame seeds by day and escorted men to visit a sacred prostitute by night—all the while singing his irrepressible songs of realization.

"Like Tilopa grinding the sesame seeds to get the sesame oil as an analogy for becoming enlightened," I say smartly.

Perhaps I say it a bit too smartly.

"Something like that," he says again with noticeably less feeling. This particular conversation has definitely reached its end. And as always in being with him, there seems to be little or no ground for knowing what might come next. We continue to sit in silence for what seems a very long time. He picks up his glass of sake with excruciating deliberateness, sips it even more slowly, places it back down on his side table with a gesture that seems to take hours.

I begin to feel that familiar and not entirely welcome sensation of falling through vast space in his presence with nowhere to land.

"Do you know that I first met you when I was making maple syrup?" I finally blurt out.

No doubt I'm trying to maintain whatever I imagine the thread of this conversation might be. At the same time, I have the peculiar sensation that my words are requiring so much more effort to put out into the space than I would ever have anticipated.

He looks at me now as if I've just entered the room for the first time, and almost as if he's wondering who I am and how I've gotten in here.

"How so?" he asks politely.

"Well, not literally, obviously. But because you have to wait such a long while for all that sap to boil ..." I plow forward. His gaze as I speak is not unkind ... "so I would sometimes bring a book along to fill the time. One day I brought your book *Meditation in Action.* A good friend at the time had recommended it to me."

"Mm-hmm." His graceful fingers move like a geisha's to grasp the crystal glass of sake.

"I had never read anything of yours before, and reading it made me want to meet you in person," I add enthusiastically.

I can feel the warmth rising up from my chest toward my face. I want so much to tell him how much this book has meant to me; how reading it was one of the most important turning points of my whole life; how I can still remember every detail of that day in the sugarhouse by Black Falls Creek, the way the maples swayed gently in the spring breezes, the way the clouds moved, the sound of the water, the smell of the boiling sap, and most of all, the gentle humor and cutting insight infused in every page of that little orange book, which I've reread ten times at least and whose pages are held together now only by a thick, fraying rubber band …

"And so you have," he says softly.

"So I have?"

"Met me in person."

"Oh yes. Yes, of course. So I have."

I feel as if I've just woken up from a dream. I flush even more. I hope he hasn't noticed.

Of course he has. And of course he isn't keeping score, either. Remembering this, I relax a little.

"I hope you didn't get too distracted and burn the maple syrup," he says with a sly little grin, taking another long sip of sake.

Then he motions to his attendant and informs me that he needs to go to "the loo." He rises slowly, nods good-bye to me, and together they leave the room.

He walks into the big meditation hall in Boulder. Three months have passed since our conversation about maple syrup. He's wearing an olive green military uniform for this particular event, rather than white or black, colors that are reserved for more formal occasions. There are epaulettes on his shoulders and medals all over the left side of his chest and a large medallion on the center of his cap. The medals are numerous, multi-colored, and precise in their symbolism.

On close inspection, they are also without exception elegant and beautiful. He himself has designed them all. Each represents a different aspect of the Shambhala teachings of gentle warriorship. Since he envisioned the entire Shambhala world five years ago and has apparently already realized every aspect of it within himself, he also gets to wear them all.

There is the orange medal of the Tiger of Meek—mindful and humble conduct. There is the white medal of the Snow Lion of Perky—penetrating insight adorned with a playful sense of humor. There is the red medal of the Garuda of Outrageous—fearlessness in going beyond conventional expectations. There is the blue medal of the Dragon of Inscrutable—spontaneous and unfathomable wisdom beyond any deliberate effort. And there are many others, which shine and sparkle as he moves through the hall.

His teaching, communicated through his uniform, seems to be connected with Outrageous. My anxiety at the sight of him wearing all his military medals makes me slightly shaky. Though this particular manifestation of his is not unfamiliar to me, I know that almost none of the three hundred students gathered in the hall have seen him in this way. Indeed, the vast majority of them have never seen him before at all.

What they know is entirely through his books and the stories they've read or heard of his life. They know he created the curriculum for Shambhala Training, which begins with a cycle of five weekend meditation retreats (referred to as levels) through which each of them has progressed over the past few years. Now that they have all reached the highly touted fifth and final level, their anticipation is very high: It's the level that only he himself teaches. They'll finally get to meet and communicate with him directly for the first time.

What many of them probably don't know is that he has created a military service organization within the Shambhala community to safeguard the environment so that his teachings can be presented properly. He serves, naturally, as its commander, and at times of his choosing, tonight for instance, dons the uniform. This enlightened military expression also brings our fear and aversion toward the conventional military world out into the open. His further intention is to teach us that we can cultivate the enlightened aspects of military service—such as precision and discipline—while letting go of the destructive aspects, like aggression and blind obedience to authority.

But if even some of his closest students have found it hard to accept this part of his world, what will this crowd of newcomers make of it? Certainly I myself have not fully made peace yet with Rinpoche's manifestation as the Warrior General of Shambhala.

Why couldn't he have worn something less provocative this evening? A meditation master is supposed to project an image of peace and serenity, or at the very least apparel himself in civilian clothing!

Why must he always do things like this?

I feel as if I'm seeing him now through a blur of confusion and rising panic. What am I afraid of? On first examination, it seems that I'm afraid for *them*.

Even as the absurdity of this fear becomes apparent in my hypervigilant consciousness, it persists. Here I stand, actually trying to take responsibility for all these people and their reactions to this vivid display he has deliberately chosen in order to introduce himself for the first time to a room full of strangers.

Even though a part of me knows that all this is nothing but my own fear being reflected back to me, as if from a bright mirror, still I continue to take it on for everyone else. I can hear his chuckle were I to reveal it to him. No doubt I already have.

I imagine that to the students he must look like he's a wounded and disabled but highly decorated Indonesian general, rolling forward with his trademark limp in his deliberate and dignified way.

Or, in a more lurid moment of my paranoid fantasy, he morphs into a Guatemalan military dictator coming to preside over an official governmental ceremony of some kind.

But then there is also that uncanny ease and relaxation that always seems to accompany his every movement. And now the smile, which flashes in the direction of someone who before that moment was a perfect stranger and who, I can only imagine, now feels as if they know him a little. Or as if they have just been introduced directly to a secret of the training they had never realized before—some gentle and utterly disarming moment of warrior intimacy in the middle of a review of a battalion of foreign troops.

Now, I'm shocked to realize, I'm afraid for *him*!

I find myself mentally drawing a protective circle around him to shield him from any unfriendly or suspicious reactions from the crowd. My mind squirms at the inappropriateness of its projections. Why do I feel protective of *him* now? Why do I imagine that he would ever need my protection?

It's almost as if it were I myself who insisted that he upset their expectations by appearing in the most provocative guise he could think of. And now it is up to me to protect him from the repercussions.

If anything, he delights in provoking uneasiness and discomfort. It increases the long but always possible odds that someone in the room will wake up completely, right on the spot. Even myself.

Once a student asked him why he drank so much, and he replied, "Sometimes it is necessary to insult in order to communicate."

I myself am certainly feeling quite uneasy at this point, and wondering also how many students are feeling insulted. My inner claustrophobia peaks as he steps carefully up onto the little stage at the front of the hall with the help of his attendant, and sits slowly down in the chair from which he will speak.

Why such claustrophobia? Because it is my job, as administrative director of Shambhala Training, to formally introduce him to everyone. No doubt a part of me, focused on our precarious operating budget, is wondering whether students will now get up *en masse*, leave the hall, and demand their money back.

It's the post to which he himself assigned me two years earlier. It is a weighty and impressive credential for the moment—one of the first official confirmations of my existence in his world. And of course this also makes it a setup for deflation at the most unexpected times.

Earlier in the year, after we'd moved to new administrative offices, Rinpoche visited our establishment and remarked that the old meditation cushions looked quite funky by contrast and needed to be replaced.

His precise words were, in fact, "They look as if people have been coming on them for years."

With this pointed encouragement, we not only purchased an entire inventory of brand new meditation cushions, but also redesigned the entire training space with his help and oversight. At last, and after seemingly endless fine-tuning, we invited him to our grand opening and requested that he bless the premises. He hobbled slowly from room to room, finally seating himself behind the desk in my office. Not a single offending object occupied its polished surface.

Indeed, the entire office was spotless, like every other nook and cranny of the space. Nothing anywhere was out of place. It was as if we had decided that he were the head camp counselor, inspecting our camper tents to make sure the beds had been made properly and the floors had been swept clean of every particle of dust. One of his calligraphies, executed by him at our request for this very office and framed in the most rich and tasteful way we could manage, glowed from the wall above the desk.

I stood in the doorway, looking at him expectantly, as if he might now award me a small ribbon for how impeccably pristine the national office of Shambhala Training looked. Behind me stood my colleagues, craning their necks in hopes they might see whatever I was seeing.

He opened the top drawer of the desk and looked at its contents for a puzzlingly long time. I asked if there was something I could get for him.

"You seem to be very proud of your handiwork," he replied, looking piercingly up at me.

Then he removed a large paper clip from the drawer, and placed it on his lower lip.

Now, as he settles into yet another chair, I turn to the huge audience and begin to tell them pretty much everything I know about him.

I have rehearsed the introduction several times and hold a small index card lest I forget anything. To alleviate my anxiety, I begin to hold forth rapidly and voluminously. It is as if the more I fill the space with words of praise, the less anyone will notice that he is sitting up there in a full military uniform with enough medals to intimidate even the Joint Chiefs of Staff.

I tell them how he was empowered as abbot of his monastery at the age of eight, how and when he left Tibet, how he came to America, how he moved to Boulder because the Rocky Mountains reminded him of the world of his youth, how he founded Naropa Institute here nearly ten years before, how he envisioned this very program, Shambhala Training, as a way to bring ancient wisdom to the modern world, and how he …

The restless movement in the audience sends me the message that I am probably going on a bit too long. I look over at him. He appears to have fallen asleep.

I make a hasty executive decision at this ambiguous juncture to round out what has begun to sound more like a eulogy than an introduction. I then pivot smoothly into the traditional supplication from student to teacher in the Buddhist tradition. Looking directly at him, I pronounce rather dramatically:

"And now sir, on behalf of all the apprentice warriors gathered here this evening, I request you to turn the wheel of the Shambhala teachings for the benefit of all of us."

He seems to stir slightly in his chair, and looking back in my general direction, replies in a strong, clear voice:

*"Turn it yourself!"*

There is a gap.

I am confused. Is he saying that he wants me to give this talk? But I'm not ready! My heart begins to race alarmingly. Apparently he has said this quite loudly, because in an instant the entire hall seems to erupt into uncontrollable laughter. I feel vertigo. The floor of the hall seems frighteningly distant. I look down at the polished hardwood floorboards to see if there might be a trapdoor at my feet that I have not noticed before, and through which I might beat a hasty retreat. Not so. There is no escape.

The laughter seems to continue beyond any reasonable duration. I have no choice, finally, but to join in the general merriment at my expense. Then I sit down, grateful for my relative invisibility at last. At least I don't have to give the talk! Someone claps my shoulder sympathetically.

"Good morning, ladies and gentlemen." He begins in his accustomed way, no matter what time of day or—more usually—night.

"Perhaps this might be somewhat surprising to you, but it is always morning for the warriors of Shambhala," he continues.

He pauses to drink from the glass on the side table next to him, taking in the whole audience with his gaze as he sips.

"And that is because the sun of awake is always rising in our heart, and in our life altogether. That is always possible. And that is why we call it the Great Eastern Sun."

He looks out at the gathering with a smile so sweet, so unbearably tender, that the cognitive dissonance it makes with his military uniform is hallucinatory. He picks up a ceremonial lacquered scepter from the side table and raises it in his right hand.

"I am *Lord Mukpo*," he continues, enunciating his family name with special emphasis and waving the scepter gracefully back and forth with a gentle flourish.

In spite of myself, I glance out at the crowd when he utters the word *Lord*. Is anyone doing a skeptical double take at this strange Tibetan personage who speaks like a British aristocrat and has now apparently appropriated a title usually bestowed only by the Queen herself?

As I hurriedly label this fearful little mental impulse "thinking" and clear my mind again, he continues.

"In the conventional way of speaking, a lord is someone who lords it over other people. But in this case, in my own case, if I may say so, a lord is someone who promotes the lordship in every person I meet."

It is as if the whole space takes an outbreath. The room relaxes completely as one huge person. He stops for what seems a long while, places the scepter down, and sips again from the sparkling crystal glass on the side table by his chair. It's sake. I can smell it from where I sit.

I no longer care. There is nothing any longer to protect.

Like the others around me, I let myself expand into his presence, like sitting in a sauna as it begins to warm up. Of course, this is Lord Mukpo, and one of the costumes such a lord chooses to display to the world at times is military. Of course it is.

The last traces of paranoia dissolve. I surrender—for the thousandth time—to his world.

"This has nothing to do with titles or riches or such things—nothing at all. Nothing whatsoever. It has to do with the dignity of being a lord—or lady for that matter—in your own world. It has to do with trust in your own fundamental goodness, confidence in that."

He pauses again, looking very, very slowly around the room, as if to search each face to see if it understands what is being said.

"Some kind of pride, without any arrogance. Or even some kind of arrogance in the most positive sense, ladies and gentlemen. Some kind of regal feeling, we could say quite definitely—that you are a human being and that your life is worth living."

His voice has become almost breathless with exhilaration. His smile could disarm anything. It has all become so simple and so penetrating, so direct and heartfelt. So ... himself!

I feel such happiness that he is already giving them what they came for, and more, whether they even know it yet or not. It is as if he is already presiding over their coronation. My embarrassment at my public humiliation a few short minutes ago fades. He says something funny and I join in the laughter.

It is not until several years later that I realize he has just—in that moment of excruciating public exposure—

bestowed upon me one of the greatest empowerments of my life, as he will soon ask me to teach and represent him personally on my own for the first time.

# Chapter 12

Standing in the front yard of the house Helen and I are renting in Berkeley, my mother gives a childlike exclamation of joy.

"I think I'll use these," she says.

She cuts a few bright yellow tiger lilies in full bloom by the white picket fence. I have lived here for less than a year, sent by Rinpoche to teach the dharma and guide the Shambhala meditation center a mile down the road.

"Oh, and these!" she exclaims, bending over a lemon bush with fully ripe yellow globes of fruit on some of its branches, and not-yet ripe green ones on others. She snips a few of each, cuts some stalks of fresh, young bamboo by the back porch, and puts all of her trophies carefully in a large white plastic bucket filled with water.

My mother and father are visiting me here for the first time.

And by a confluence of what the Tibetans call *tendrel*—auspicious coincidence—Rinpoche is visiting the meditation center this same weekend. He is here to teach an advanced intensive training program. And by a further auspicious coincidence, it's also my birthday. This evening our community will greet Rinpoche with an exhibition and performances of artistic work of various kinds—paintings, sculptures, photographs, poetry, music, weavings, and flower arrangements. The entire circumference of the meditation hall is filled with these offerings from his earnest and devoted students.

My mother, though not deeply trained in the art of flower arranging, wants very much to make her own offering for the occasion. She has been an avid and very competent gardener since my early childhood, and is never happier than when working in her garden, her hands in the soil, lovingly planting beds of flowers every spring.

"There. What do you think?" she turns and asks my father.

They are standing together now in the meditation hall an hour or so before the start of the exhibition. The lemon branches and tiger lilies from our front yard are now arranged in rich profusion in a dark green ceramic ikebana container.

"It's fine," says my father approvingly but with a hint of impatience. "Don't fuss with it so much. It's fine just as it is."

My mother moves one of the tiger lilies in the vase again, like a girl brushing hair out of her eyes. She stands back, appraises it once more, then lets it be …

"Who did this one?" asks Rinpoche, his gentle, high-pitched voice radiating into the hall an hour later. He's been moving from one piece to another, stopping briefly at times, often not pausing at all as he slowly circles the big room. He is dressed elegantly in a dark suit; his tie shines with its pattern of black and gold. As the head of the center I walk beside him, also in a dark suit, feeling more relaxed and at ease than I generally do in his presence, as if he and I are sharing a secret.

We are standing in front of my mother's flower arrangement. He makes a very definite stop there and looks at it appraisingly. How could he have known? Merely coincidence, I hastily remind myself. Don't make a mystical big deal out of all this.

"I did," my mother calls out perkily from the other side of the room. Rinpoche turns slowly in the direction of her voice. Now she has her hand up, like a schoolgirl waiting to be called upon to give the right answer. He looks at her without speaking, and then beckons to her with his index finger. She walks over to him, standing now to his left as I stand to his right.

"Sir, this is my mother," I say.

"Hello."

Rinpoche looks at my mother and smiles with disarming warmth and kindness. This is their first meeting in person. She seems to melt a little, and then gathers herself together again to speak.

"Hello, I'm so happy to meet you, Rinpoche. Is it Rinpoche? Did I pronounce it right?" She becomes a little flustered. He smiles again and nods in the affirmative.

"What inspired you to make this?" he asks.

"I wanted to offer a gift for my son and his wife in their new home here, and on his birthday," she answers confidently. "All the materials for the arrangement were growing right in the yard of their home."

"Mm-hmm," Rinpoche listens, looking at her intently. I can feel her become a little self-conscious again, but she continues gamely.

"California has so many beautiful flowers at every time of year," she effuses.

"Yes," he agrees. He turns back to her flower arrangement and studies it for a few moments.

"Do you have any suggestions for me? About the arrangement, I mean," my mother asks, as if she wants to grasp every possible thread of meaning from this long-awaited encounter.

Then Rinpoche turns to me and asks me to bring him the *ikebana* clippers, which are lying on a nearby table. I fetch them for him. He turns again to my mother.

"May I?" he asks her with exquisite courtesy.

She nods her consent. He turns to her arrangement, clippers in hand. He snips here, then there, then there, maybe half a dozen swift cuts in all. After each one, I catch the severed branch and put it aside. In no more than a minute, he is finished.

My mother looks at his handiwork. Her eyes are wide with amazement. The yellow tiger lilies gleam out into the room, freed from behind their veil. The yellow and green globes of fruit on the lemon branches glow like colored glass balls on a Christmas tree. They too have been set completely free to shine as themselves. Around them the green bamboo foliage rises gracefully up to support them without crowding them any longer.

Rinpoche hands the clippers back to me.

"How did you do that?" my mother asks him. Her voice is charged with wonder and astonishment.

"I think it's just a matter of opening things up a little," he answers.

"Opening things up?"

"Yes," he says. He touches my mother's hand tenderly. "Flowers are like children. They do best when you give them plenty of space."

*Chögyam Trungpa Rinpoche, 1979. Photograph by Michael Wood.*

Next day is my birthday. We invite Rinpoche to come to our home for dinner. He sends his regrets through his attendant, saying that the weekend teaching schedule won't quite accommodate it. In turn, he invites Helen and me, along with my parents, to his suite at the meditation center—my own office, actually—to join him for tea during a break in the program.

Though my father has seen Rinpoche several times over the previous eight years, they have never met. He sits next to my mother on the slightly threadbare sofa in the office.

Rinpoche sits across from them in the most dignified chair we can find for the occasion. Through Helen's skilled efforts, my office looks for the moment as elegant as it ever will during our time in Berkeley. His attendant offers my parents some tea. My mother accepts enthusiastically; my father asks if it might be possible to get some coffee.

"You are a doctor," Rinpoche begins the conversation.

My father seems pleased that Rinpoche knows this, and relieved that he now has something to talk about. He mentions that his medical practice for nearly forty years has been with children, and that his work now is to deliver care to poor black families in the inner city of Waterbury, Connecticut. Rinpoche nods politely and sips his tea.

He continues, "And you know a great deal about birds as well."

My father smiles. "My son must have told you," he says.

"Actually, *my* son told me," Rinpoche replies.

My father looks slightly puzzled. I am amazed myself at the details Rinpoche seems always to have at his command when the appropriate situation presents itself, and remind my father of the morning six summers ago when he and I woke at dawn to go bird watching with Rinpoche's oldest son and dharma heir, Ösel.

"Oh yes, of course," my father smiles. "Your son had very keen eyes, I remember. And strong legs—it was hard for me to keep up with him."

Rinpoche smiles. "It was kind of you to take an interest in him like that," he says.

"Well, you know," says my father. "Bird-watchers are an endangered species themselves these days. I was happy to see how interested he was, and I'm glad that he enjoyed it."

Rinpoche nods again without smiling and sips his tea.

I can feel that my father is struggling slightly with the unfamiliar force field of Rinpoche's presence. On the one hand, there seems to be a definite sense of invitation for him to hold forth in his accustomed way, filling the room with his charm and personality. On the other, there seems to be no real invitation at all. He falls silent and swallows his coffee.

"How do you feel about what your son is doing here in Berkeley?" Rinpoche asks my father suddenly.

"I've always told Frank that whatever makes him happy makes me happy," replies my father, not entirely convincingly. Rinpoche motions to his attendant to offer everyone more tea.

"You must be quite proud of your son," he continues.

"I'm very proud of all of my children," my father answers, almost defiantly. "Only one of them—my daughter—became a doctor, but I'm proud of all of them."

Rinpoche says nothing. Turning to his attendant, he whispers something. The attendant leaves the room and returns moments later with a large bouquet of white chrysanthemums. Rinpoche gestures in my direction, and the attendant presents me with the fresh white flowers. There are a dozen of them, and their stems are uncommonly long. I hold them awkwardly in my lap.

"Rinpoche wishes you a cheerful birthday," the attendant says solemnly with just a hint of a grin. He steps back. "And he has also composed a birthday poem for you in honor of the occasion." Reaching into his jacket pocket, the attendant takes out a folded piece of paper, unfolds it, and begins reading:

"The poem is titled 'The Smile of Peonies.'

"Challenge is like witnessing red peony flowers for the first time
Seeing the Great Eastern Sun is shocking and beloved."

My mother's eyes are already moist. She seems to be staring at the chrysanthemums.

"I appreciate your brilliance and goodness."

Did I actually hear that line being read just now in this room? I begin to feel slightly dizzy. Will I get a copy of this later? Will that line still be there if I do?

"Be a tiger
Be a rock
Be a typhoon."

I gaze at the wall of my office, behind Rinpoche's chair and above his head. Hanging there is a gift I received shortly after I arrived here—a print of a fierce Mongolian warrior on a white horse soaring through space, his bow drawn tight, the arrow ready to fly to its target. Overwhelmed, I focus my own eyes resolutely on the sharp tip of that arrow.

"I appreciate your service.
May you live long,
May you have a happy life,
I trust you and I adore you."

The attendant folds the paper again and puts it in his pocket. He assures me that I will receive a formal copy before the weekend is over. Then Rinpoche offers me a little bow. I bow in return, but I am in a mellow haze, and my thinking mind has dissolved altogether.

At this moment my mother suddenly gets up from the sofa and goes over to Rinpoche. Her eyes are wet with tears. She kneels in front of him and takes his right hand between her hands. She thanks him for everything she can think of, then returns to her seat next to my father.

Rinpoche takes one more sip of his tea. He turns toward my father, "I want to thank you for educating your son so well," he says firmly.

He takes one final sip of tea. Then, with a slight bow that is both gracious and utterly unyielding, he says:

"And today I also want to thank you for turning his education fully over to me."

# Chapter 13

It is 1984, only a year later, but whatever honeymoon I might have had, not only in my marriage but also with the dharma community in Berkeley, is definitely over.

Helen and I fight incessantly about everything, especially money—about how there isn't enough and that it's the fault of the people here for being so ungenerous. After all, we've uprooted our whole lives to come out here, and not only that, it wasn't even our idea. It was Rinpoche's idea. Why can't people here see that! Why don't they give us a bigger parsonage? Look at what Randy in New York gets. We should have been asked to go to New York.

We go on and on in this way. Sometimes I repeat the litany, sometimes she does. In moments of relative calm, I try to play the devil's advocate against our own arguments:

There aren't as many people here, and they don't have a lot of money, number one.

Number two, I'm the third director sent from elsewhere that they've been asked to support in the past ten years, and it's quite possible they're getting pretty tired of it.

We uprooted our whole lives long before now, even in deciding to study with Rinpoche, number three. To claim that this time is somehow more worthy of sympathy than all the other times seems slightly disingenuous.

And number four, the way we fight all the time—it's really no wonder that people don't want to give us a lot of support! We're probably an embarrassment to them.

Helen will have none of it. She states her case clearly and without compromise.

"I don't care what the people here think. I was happy in Boulder. We both had paying jobs that we liked. And we were near Rinpoche and could see him much more often. You were happier, too, but you don't want to admit it."

I remind her that this is precisely the point. Sooner or later we had to get kicked out of the nest. How many times had he told us this? How many times had he himself experienced it? Did he ever ask any of his students to do anything that he himself hadn't done a hundred times first?

"The whole thing is a test," I proclaim righteously.

"What are you talking about? What kind of test?"

"A test of whether we're truly willing to live the vows we've taken with him."

"Don't be so pious," she retorts acidly.

"Pious? What does that have to do with it?"

"The problem is that you're much too religious, otherwise we would never have gotten into this mess. You would have seen that New York was a better situation. I hate this place. It's just a bunch of aging hippies."

Ah, so that's the real problem—I'm too religious! I'm an enlightenment fundamentalist. As always, there's a painfully accurate insight within her resentment.

There's nothing more to be gained from this conversation. I slam the door and drive up into the hills to look at the ocean and lick my wounds. Looking out at the Golden Gate glistening in the distance like a cruel mirage, I ponder my predicament.

Memory transports me to the living room of Rinpoche's house in Boulder eighteen months before, the morning he asked me if I would consider going to Berkeley to represent him to the community there.

Of course, I am honored and even flattered. But pained at the same time. The window of his living room is open to the cool morning air. Birds sing exuberantly in the big shade trees outside. I am so happy here. In some ways, being asked to do this feels like a kind of exile. I'm being banished somehow from his presence. He tells me to think about it and take my time.

A few weeks later, I meet with him again to tell him that I will go.

"That's good," he says simply.

"I will miss you."

"That's good, too." He smiles at me.

"How should I regard this assignment, sir?" I ask him, trying to control my emotionality with a more professional approach.

He considers the question for a moment, and says, "You should think of yourself as a diplomat visiting a foreign country."

"Foreign?"

"Yes."

"How so?"

"You are an ambassador representing the Kingdom of Shambhala, and California is a foreign country."

"Oh, I see."

"Don't be overly ambitious."

"In what way?"

"Because it's a foreign country. The Shambhala world will never really take root there."

Responding to my obvious expression of disappointment, he adds, "But you can have a very helpful dialogue with people."

"Why won't Shambhala ever really take root there?"

"The situation is a little too comfortable, too sleepy in some sense."

"How will dialogue with people help, then?"

"There are good people everywhere who can connect. It is not a problem with individuals. But the larger environment will not be that fertile."

"I see."

"We will have to plow that field elsewhere."

"You mean Nova Scotia?" Already there are rumors that he will soon move to Halifax to live, and establish the capital of Shambhala there.

"Yes, indeed!"

He smiles almost gleefully. His eyes shine and his whole body seems ready to fly joyfully from his chair. Outside the window, the morning birdsong seems to hit a sudden manic crescendo. I have the uncannily familiar feeling that he is orchestrating our reality in this moment, so that every element of the phenomenal world is conspiring to impress upon me the point he is making in a way that transcends any possible objection.

As it turns out, so he is. Otherwise I wouldn't find myself now sitting on top of this hill looking out at the Golden Gate and mulling the apparent hopelessness of my situation. I must talk to him about all this next time I see him, though what exactly I might say to him is something of a mystery.

Don't try so hard, I remind myself ...

A few weeks later, he is listening patiently as I review the litany of our sufferings here in Berkeley.

"When we first got here, I could do no wrong. Everybody thought I was doing a great job back then."

"Mm-hmm."

"Those days are long gone."

He chuckles softly. I have the growing sense that I may be making too big a deal of all this.

"Now I seem to be getting criticized on all sides. I realize how much I just want people to like me. Their criticism makes me very defensive."

"Mm-hmm."

"And Helen is so unhappy. She doesn't like it here at all."

"Mm-hmm."

We sit in silence for a while. Rinpoche rubs his jaw.

"There is always truth in other people's criticisms of oneself," he says at last, almost as if he were speaking about himself rather than me.

"Always," he repeats meaningfully. "Even when their motivation is not completely clean in doing so. It doesn't really matter all that much, actually."

Then his tongue rolls in a leisurely arc inside his cheek. He looks at me closely.

"You must open yourself up further in order to see that, and find out what that truth is exactly and how it can be helpful."

I nod dutifully.

"Your wanting to be liked is also a problem. It undermines your strength."

The feedback is excruciating. I suddenly flash on one of his phrases from years before—that studying with a spiritual master is like having an operation without anesthetics. I feel as though I'm bleeding onto the floor between us.

"At the same time, you must rely on your own practice and your own understanding in the end. The criticism of others is never the last word."

"In what sense?"

"It is simply helpful in pointing out your arrogance and your blind spots. But that is just the beginning. The rest is up to you."

"What do I do then at that point?"

His patience seems endless in this moment. He takes me in with a look of sadness, but says fiercely:

*"You must make your whole life into no complaint."*

There are no further questions I can possibly ask. I thank him and rise to leave. As I reach the door, I hear him say that a sense of humor is always a saving grace.

Suddenly it begins to rain out of a clear blue sky.

It is a torrential rain. It is all the more shocking, and uncannily strange, in that it is descending from a heaven without a cloud anywhere to be seen.

At the moment it begins, I am marching. I have spent the last week camping and drilling as a fresh civilian recruit, invited by Rinpoche to attend the annual summer military encampment high in the Rockies for the first, and only, time.

There are perhaps a dozen of us, sprinkled among the hundred or so military veterans of the Shambhala community who gather here every summer. The experience has been far less intimidating than I anticipated. Rugged and strenuous in its own way, yes, but full of playfulness and humor, like Rinpoche himself. One could probably say that it is like a gathering of Buddhist Boy Scouts.

Before the rain starts, the midday sun is intense. We march together in an open field, with a traditional Japanese torii gate at one end and Rinpoche's tent at the other, no more than a hundred yards away. I am sweating and uncomfortable, but strangely exhilarated.

Though this march is in no sense a formal review, Rinpoche is sitting out in front of his tent on a canvas director's chair, dressed in khakis and holding a lacquered scepter of some kind in his hand. Next to him sits another man, apparently an honored visitor. We later learn that it is a Native American medicine man who has come to pay his respects, and to whom Rinpoche, with characteristic humbleness, is in turn paying his own.

And then the rain begins.

It is a deluge of almost biblical intensity. It drives us off the parade ground immediately. We take refuge in the large meditation tent adjoining the field, but the rain is so heavy that it begins to flood the area under the tent. In moments we are working with frantic efficiency as one, moving all the meditation cushions to a higher platform near the center of the tent, digging trenches to divert the flooding water around its edges.

In minutes, the rain subsides to a tender, misty drizzle. The sky is still as clear as when the first drops fell. Someone calls excitedly to us as we haul the last cushions to the platform.

We look out. From the crown of the torii gate into the very center of Rinpoche's tent, there is a perfect tiny rainbow. It shimmers brilliantly in the luminous mist, seeming to grow more vivid by the moment. Behind it, the dark green needles of the pines on the edge of the parade ground glitter in the sun like precious jewels.

Later we hear from others that just after that rain, there was an even tinier rainbow over the entrance gate of the retreat center, half a mile away.

I gaze now at the empty chairs in front of Rinpoche's tent. Like a magical illusion, he has vanished.

We can begin to feel him leaving, more and more.

Not just this country, which he obviously no longer sees as the focal point of the work he has to do while he is still here on the earth, but this human world altogether. This realization fills me with a growing panic, and sadness, too.

Already he spends more and more of his time communing with an unimaginably pure and potent (but to us, still invisible) world of energies and elemental forces—the sacred world of the gods, or *dralas*. From the start, he has made it quite clear to us that it is only through the existence and blessings of these dralas that he has gained access to Shambhala.

Because they are his access, and because he in turn is our access, it is more and more obvious that the dralas are of indispensable importance to everything we're doing together.

Earlier on, it seemed he would visit the dralas for short, pregnant periods and return with new spiritual offspring each time. Now, it seems that he spends most of his time playing or conversing with them, awake or asleep. That persistent ambiguity about his humanness in any conventional sense of the word—those ordinary qualities that link him to us and to our visible world—becomes more and more heightened. He spends most of his life now in a place to which we cannot accompany him or even follow him.

I travel from my post in Berkeley to Halifax to see him where he now lives. He gives a public talk at the medical school of Dalhousie University, sitting in a simple chair in the operating amphitheater of one of the surgical training rooms while an audience of hundreds fills the seats all around and above him.

He speaks about familiar things—the importance of creating an enlightened society, the need for greater kindness in the human world, the decency of what already exists here in Nova Scotia as a fertile ground for the dharma to take root and flourish over many coming generations. The more I listen, the more I realize that he is not coming back to America again except to visit us and, if anything, urge us to move here.

I think about the logistical challenges of uprooting my life in order to be closer to him. I consider the inconvenient fact that I'm still serving in California at his express wish and command—"a diplomat in a foreign country."

I begin to feel increasingly lonely and cut off from him—something I have not experienced in his presence now for several years. It is something that I naïvely thought I'd finally outgrown, as if my loneliness were somehow a weakness. Clumsily, and in reaction to these uncomfortable feelings, I raise my hand after his talk. He looks up into the audience and makes a gesture in my direction with his right hand.

"Sir, for those of us who feel deeply about the things you are describing tonight, but who live many thousands of miles away from you, how would you suggest we could best share your vision now?"

Will I never learn? Scarcely have I finished the question when I see him taking off his eyeglasses and holding them up toward me.

"Perhaps you should borrow my spectacles," he replies. Peals of laughter fill the hall. He puts his glasses on again and gestures graciously toward the next question.

That autumn, he comes to California for what will be the last time. Meeting in the living room of a private home with a small group of his closest students in the Bay Area community, his face is gaunt, his expression is wrathful, his complexion dark as basalt. Every word from him has the weight and conviction of clairvoyant prophecy:

"This country will become unrecognizable to you in the next twenty-five years. There will be crises and challenges of all kinds—the economy, the climate, politics, the spiritual scene. There will be huge ups and downs financially and in terms of livelihood. It will create great suffering for many people. There will be extremes of climate—fires, floods, earthquakes, unlike anything in the past.

"There will be much more fear, which politicians will take advantage of. There will be much less hospitality for spiritual views and practices that are seen to be outside the mainstream. There will be a rise of religious fundamentalism throughout the United States. You will feel more and more as if you're living in a third-world country."

He leans forward, peering at us with great intensity. His certainty is at once terrifying and oddly comforting.

"You must each make every effort to move to Nova Scotia and help with our work there in establishing the Kingdom of Shambhala. There is no time to waste. No time at all."

He offers us a gentle, closing bow, and gets up to go to bed.

Next morning his attendants rise early to take him to the airport. We line up around his waiting car to say good-bye.

"I love you, Rinpoche," says my friend Eamon to him as he helps him into the car.

Eamon and his wife Michelle have made their home available to Rinpoche as a residence for many years whenever he has come to Berkeley to teach. At those times, their house is referred to, simply, as the Court. Even in the years after Rinpoche's last visit there, all of us will still call their house by that name. And it will still carry the dignity of his presence, like an empty perfume bottle.

"I love you all," Rinpoche replies with a huge smile, taking in all our heartbroken expressions as we stand in a circle around his car, even in front of it, as if we would restrain it from leaving.

For most of us there, it is the last time we will ever see him.

# Chapter 14

What does it actually mean to fall in love with a Buddha? And what is it about this love that makes it different somehow from any other?

In the thirteen years that I knew my teacher while he was alive, and in all the years since, this question has haunted me and continues to do so. I doubt that there is any final answer to such a question. But here is what I think I understand about it so far.

It is the unique quality of a Buddha that each interaction with him or her provokes the potential for illumination—right on the spot. The experience of illumination can be likened to seeing yourself in a clear mirror. The mirror is perfectly clear because the Buddha has absolutely no agenda other than to be fully genuine and to wake you up to your own genuineness.

The genuineness of a Buddha is an expression of utter fearlessness, because there are no second thoughts in a Buddha's mind about how to relate to others. There are no second thoughts because a Buddha has nothing to defend, to protect, or to lose. This state of complete fearlessness is something that ordinary people experience only rarely, if ever.

We have no other relationships in life that function in quite this way. Our friends, family, lovers, even enemies may mirror us to a certain extent, but the reflection they provide is not perfectly clear. They bring their own agendas of confusion, projection, and conflicting emotions to their encounters with us, as we do with them.

Because the mirrors they provide are not completely clear, we may end up reading whatever we wish to read from our encounters with them, or even ignoring the clarity that is there, and that could help us if we were open to it.

With a Buddha, however, the mirror is utterly clear, and the messages unambiguous.

*The first stage of falling in love with a Buddha is embarrassment.*

The embarrassment comes from having our confusion and shortcomings so clearly exposed. We cannot argue with such a mirror, because it is so accurate and direct, and entirely without ulterior motives. At times we experience this mirror as merciless because it is so uncompromising. It is not so much that a Buddha is deliberately trying to embarrass us, but that the pristine clarity of the reflection is hard for us to look at without turning away. When we see our grasping, our pride, our insecurities so vividly displayed, it is excruciating.

As a result, we may often have very strong feelings of anxiety or resistance to being in the presence of such a mirror. Indeed, we may want to run away and never come back. For many, this is what happens. But if we are able to move beyond our embarrassment, we may enter the second stage of falling in love with a Buddha. Indeed, Chögyam Trungpa Rinpoche liked to say that the experience of disappointment was the most reliable, and valuable, one we could possibly have in growing spiritually. It cut through our wishful thinking, and helped us see things more clearly and more realistically.

*The next stage is longing.*

This longing arises, first of all, because the love that a Buddha expresses toward us is unconditional. No matter how little affection we may have for ourselves at any moment, a Buddha's affection for us is unwavering. At times this warmth—which radiates in our direction for no discernible reason and often does not seem connected in any way with how worthy we may feel we are—is overwhelming. It is like the sun, which does not discriminate where it will shine and where it will not. And like flowers, we turn toward the sun.

This longing is deepened by something further—the glimpses we have of our own enlightened potential when we are in a Buddha's presence. In a Buddha's continuous and seemingly effortless expression of his or her enlightened qualities, we glimpse our own best possibilities. What are these? They include bravery, gentleness, loving-kindness, compassion, humbleness, clear vision, cheerfulness, tireless enthusiasm, humor, patience, joy, equanimity, and uncannily skillful action in relating to challenging life situations of all kinds.

When we see these qualities clearly manifest in our teacher, we can never get enough of them. It is as if we would like to steal them and have them for ourselves. As Rinpoche himself once said, we would like to jump inside the teacher's brain and heart and live there all the time, looking out and seeing the world as he or she sees it.

Altogether, this second aspect of longing is the actual, felt experience of falling in love with a Buddha. Traditionally this longing is referred to by the term *devotion.* It is said by all the great spiritual masters that devotion is the single most important factor in a student's progress on the path toward realization.

This longing, or devotion, acts as a magnetic force equal to the power of the force of our resistance and embarrassment. This dance between resistance and longing characterizes the whole journey of relating to a Buddha as mirror, from beginning to end. We want to run away from the mirror with every fiber of our being, but we want to run toward it at the same time.

By staying with this dance of opposing forces, we learn, grow up, and become genuine warriors—brave and gentle human beings. It is a bittersweet journey, bitter in the way the mirror keeps showing us with devastating accuracy how stuck we are in our absurd preoccupations with who we think we are, yet sweet in the realization that this mirror is nothing other than unconditional love, and that its qualities are nothing other than our *own* true nature as Buddha, inseparable from our teacher's nature.

This bittersweet aspect cuts even deeper. It permeates our attitude toward the teacher's unconditional love itself. Even there, we experience a conflict between our longing for that love and our fear—even our terror—at receiving it.

We fear this love without conditions because it takes us so far beyond our familiar world and our habitual patterns. It invites us into an open space that is impervious to our bargains or games. Because this unconditional love is inseparable from the mirror the teacher is always holding up to us, there is no place to hide.

*The final stage is realizing that the Buddha is everywhere.*

What this means, first of all, is that falling in love with a Buddha is an unending love affair. Beyond that, it is an *unrequited* love affair. It is unrequited, not because a Buddha ever actually rejects us in any way, but simply because a Buddha's ultimate function is to keep reminding us that we must do the work of becoming a Buddha ourselves. There will be no final confirmation of our enlightenment from our teacher. There will be no one to congratulate us at the spiritual finish line. In fact, there will be no finish line!

A Buddha reminds us, again and again, that to become fully awakened we must fully embrace our utter *aloneness*, just as he or she has done. And paradoxically, the more alone we become, the more deeply connected we become with others.

This, we could say, is the enlightened significance and purpose of the unrequited love affair with a Buddha. In fact, the unrequitedness itself is nothing other than the real truth of what it means to love and be loved unconditionally. If we do not learn to embrace it, we may very well have completely missed the point of our relationship with our teacher! We can never make the awakened state—or the Buddha—our property or territory. We are left alone, ultimately, to taste our own hearts.

The whole principle of the guru is directly connected with the realization that the Buddha is everywhere. The word *guru* literally means "that which points toward." The guru keeps pointing us toward our own enlightened potential by effortlessly reflecting back to us both our confusion and our wisdom in every encounter.

Eventually the outer guru, in the form of our living teacher, becomes the inner guru, in the form of our encounters with every life situation. At that point, a Buddha hands us completely over to the world, so to speak. The whole world becomes our mirror, reflecting our confusion and wisdom. Now the teacher is always with us. In fact, we cannot get the Buddha out of our system even if we try. This world continues as our teacher long after our relationship with our personal teacher may have ended—whether through death or other kinds of permanent separation.

Every life experience reminds us to wake up, to be kind, to drop our self-importance, to help others, and to enjoy our lives and all our relationships without anxiety and attachment.

It seems to me that this is the endless blessing of such a love, and that the power of that blessing can never be diminished. Even by death.

# Part Three: Farewell to the Fathers

# Chapter 15

"I am His Majesty's ambassador to Berkeley."

How absurd and overstated it sounds in this charged silence! Did I think that this uniformed attendant on the porch of this big house would try to block my way if I didn't proclaim my credentials in this inflated manner? What exactly was I thinking?

Graciously, and without a word, the guard ushers me toward the entrance. With a rueful, self-mocking smile that only I can see, I reflect at how my teacher is always looking at me—in every moment, in every situation, and no matter where I go or in what direction I turn.

This thought is especially haunting at the moment, because he died two days ago, on the fourth of April, 1987, and his body is in the room just beyond this cold, misty porch in Nova Scotia. But it also feels quite definitely that *he* is in there, just as it has always felt in entering the world of his presence.

Now I can see the windows of the big room, open to the night air, and the bright light of the interior flashing in orderly rectangles out onto the dark floor of the porch where I stand. Now I can smell the pungent odor of juniper burning on large, glowing coals in the big, black cast-iron censer at the room's entrance. Now I can hear the sounds of his students, my friends, chanting the sacred songs of Shambhala that he composed for us, to remind us of what our real connection with him was, is, and will always be. Now I can taste the salt drifting in from the harbor on the chilly night air of Halifax.

And now I can feel the overwhelming sadness, and at the same time the penetrating sharpness, of the atmosphere here at Lord Mukpo's Court, his home and the blazing secret center of his world.

Rinpoche is dead.
Rinpoche is alive.
Rinpoche is dead.

This alternation of realities begins that night—first in my senses and then in my heart of hearts—and it continues to this day. I suspect that it will continue 'til the day I die. I enter the room with head bowed—as much out of embarrassment that others have certainly heard my grandiose announcement of my arrival as out of respect and devotion to my beloved teacher—and find an open meditation cushion near the rear. I look up at last toward the front.

There he is. On a throne of satin, beneath a rich, multi-colored canopy of satin and brocade, dressed in royal robes, he sits in his primordial dignity. His complexion is very dark, his face an exquisitely fine sculpture of bone beneath the tightly drawn dark flesh. His mouth still so full and sensual, his hair so black, his head turned slightly to the side and upward, his teeth bared. Looking in one moment as if he is caught permanently in a burst of cosmic laughter, and in another as if he is passionately kissing space itself. Later, we learn that the area around his heart remained warm for five days after his breathing stopped.

And just as when he was alive—and is he not now more alive than ever?—I cannot take my eyes off him. All around me the chanting continues:

"As we watch each petal grow we rejoice and cry,

And the tears of our crying produce future warriors,

When we finger your sword blade we become heartbroken ..."

Rinpoche is dead.
Rinpoche is alive.
Rinpoche is dead.

I look and look and look at him. From the Halifax harbor the mournful sound of a foghorn can be heard, like the elegy of a giant bagpipe in the distance. My eyes fill with tears.

"Why, with such sharpness, Rigden Father, are you not presently with us?"

Did he wink at me just now?

Rinpoche is alive.
Rinpoche is dead.
Rinpoche is alive.

In the months following Rinpoche's death I have two vivid dreams of him. In the first, I am walking in the woods and come to a fork in the path I've been following. Unsure of which way to take, I look up into a tree that stands right at this divide. Sitting in the tree is a big tiger, looking at me with fierceness and yet at the same time a smile, like a giant Cheshire cat. I look at the tiger, as if expecting it to tell me which way to go, but it gives no sign.

Then, without warning, it leaps out of the tree directly down on me, with its eyes shining and its jaws wide open to reveal its sharp white teeth. I cannot escape, though I'm terrified. Just as the tiger is upon me with its wide-open jaws, I look and see that its face is Rinpoche's face. I swoon and fall forward into its dark mouth. At that moment, I experience a sensation of bliss unlike any I have ever experienced before or since. I awake from the dream but the blissful feeling remains for a little while till I fall back to sleep.

In the second, I am attending Rinpoche in the meditation hall of the Berkeley center, as if he were walking in to give a talk and I were assisting him in my role as director and resident teacher. He is dressed sumptuously in the golden teaching robes he would often wear when giving the most profound oral teachings in formal settings. His face is radiant and smiling. I am filled with happiness to be attending him at such a moment.

Suddenly I look down and notice that he is urinating all over the floor of the hall as he walks. I panic and look around desperately for something with which to catch the urine. The only thing I can see is a large, shining brass bowl on the shrine. I run over, retrieve it, and kneel in front of him with the bowl. It seems he will never stop urinating. He fills the bowl and it begins to overflow. Even more panicked now, I look for any other container that might be available.

Then I hear him laughing. I look up and he is laughing at me uncontrollably. Then he motions to me to drink from the bowl. I hesitate for a moment, then do as he commands. The golden liquid in that bowl is sweet beyond description. He laughs and laughs and keeps peeing all over the polished floor.

In the first few years after Rinpoche's death, I remain in California, teaching at the center in Berkeley. Like a loyal samurai who has lost his shogun, I do not know what else to do but to keep serving him within the forms he created.

My financial support from the small community remains paltry. To supplement it, I sell insurance for several years, awkwardly and unhappily. I am deeply dissatisfied. Forty-four years old now—when will I ever find a way to make a living that honors the gifts I was given in my life? When will I ever marry my lofty spiritual aspirations to the reality of the world? When will I ever join heaven and earth in my own life?

My marriage, always challenging ever since we left the cloistered world of the retreat center ten years before, seems to become even more painful and obstructed. Helen and I begin to spend more and more time apart. With Rinpoche's passing, the real bond that sustained us through all our difficulties is gone. It is as if we had each always been married to him rather than to each other, and that this shared devotion became a substitute for the intimacy and commitment of a real marriage. It is obvious that we will ultimately go our separate ways. It is only a matter of time.

Two years after Rinpoche's death, his American dharma heir, his closest student and the titular leader of our community, reveals that he has AIDS. The revelation becomes a scandal. Rumors abound that he may have knowingly had unprotected sex even after learning of his condition. Our community descends into the turmoil and chaos of irreconcilable conflict. Like traumatized children who have lost their father too early and too young, we forget Rinpoche's heartfelt instructions to us. We turn on each other instead of caring for each other.

We wait impatiently for his son to lead, but he is still too young. Wisely, the youthful prince with whom I read the legends of King Arthur twelve years before distances himself from our confusion in order to gather his own strength. Later, he will emerge with his own vision and integrity as his father's Shambhala lineage successor. But for now, we flounder on our own, thrashing and biting each other in the bloody water. There is no reference point anywhere now to look to for wisdom or guidance.

I can no longer lead even the small group of dharma students here in Berkeley. No one in our community, anywhere in the country, can lead anyone else. Anything that I or anyone else may assert about how things should be is immediately met by the passionately opposing view of someone else with equal certainty in their opinion. My loneliness is at times unbearable. Ultimately I will have no choice but to let go of the person I have crafted—the one whose whole identity has been based on serving Rinpoche in this way.

During this excruciating era, I learn that the only way to lead at such times is to listen. Every other approach is a dead end. I stop talking so much and listen more and more. Partially it is mere self-preservation; I don't wish to make myself a target for anyone else's aggression. Partially it is to rein in my own habitual tendencies to judge and criticize others. But most of all, it is to help me enter through the gateway of a new way of being with people, one that has greater possibilities for kindness. If the dharma is not about kindness, then surely all of us have been wasting our time.

A year and a half after we learn of his illness, Rinpoche's brilliant dharma heir is dead.

I wonder now whether our community can even survive. I long to go into retreat.

It has been more than fifteen years since my first solitary retreat. Since then, I have gone on retreat every year for gradually longer periods. I have come to love retreat. It is the only way to taste my own heart without having to explain or justify what I feel or believe to anyone else. It is a way to draw close to my spiritual master; strangely, now that he is no longer living, I can draw close to him more easily than ever.

I stay in retreat for two months. It is winter in the Rocky Mountains. My cabin sits on an outcrop 9,000 feet above sea level. I heat it with wood. It is small but well insulated and comfortable. For those two months I do not see another human being. Only the retreat master comes within a few hundred feet of the cabin, to leave my weekly supply of food in a covered pail with a large rock on it. I am never aware of his presence. I leave the cabin only to walk to the outhouse through the deep snow, and to pick up the stash of food.

I rise at three thirty each morning. The moon, moving twice through all its phases during my retreat time, hangs nakedly night after night in a clear sky. By six I've already been meditating for several hours. Through the large window facing east, I watch the dawn spread behind a rocky hill directly before me. Then the sun emerges. The frozen air begins to warm. The silence is profound. I eat my breakfast slowly. Every bite is delicious.

As the days pass, my resistance to sitting dissolves altogether, perhaps for the first time in my life. There is simply nothing else to do. I practice into the evening, retiring to bed at nine thirty, rising at three thirty the next morning—day after day. I am doing a traditional practice I've received from Rinpoche known as a *sadhana*, which consists of visualizing a particular enlightened deity and reciting that deity's mantra. The visualization and mantra become a continuous presence, an unceasing flow. Eventually I even stop taking afternoon naps in my accustomed way. I taste a sense of wakefulness I haven't ever tasted before. My guru is so vividly present!

I think of his short life and all that he accomplished. I think of his dharma heir, who was himself such a powerful and important teacher and friend for me and for so many others. Both of them died at age forty-seven. So young! How can I be lazy now? How can I lull myself into the sleepy certainty that I still have plenty of time? There is no time for anything now but waking up, more and more. No time for anything but kindness. How fruitless to take sides! How futile to argue with others! There is no time.

On the final day of my retreat, this poem arises in my heart, and I write it down:

Frank W. Berliner

## Song of Devotion

To the incomparable father guru, the fiercely compassionate one,
To you whose kindness I can never repay,
To you, Chökyi Gyatso, I prostrate again and again.
From this lonely rock I cry to you,
I supplicate you to remain forever in my heart.

The face of the morning sun is cheerful and familiar,
The stars are steadfast in the vast night sky,
But you are gone, and your heart son too is gone,
The ashes of dear dharma friends disperse on this very hill,
Grant your blessing that I may truly take impermanence to heart.

In the beginning, thoughts of the past steal up behind me,
In the middle, thoughts of the present crowd around me,
At the end, thoughts of the future rush in to meet me,
Grant your blessing that I may tame this wandering mind once more.

The clouds delight with their dissolving dance,
The moon beguiles with her ebb and flow of light,

The crystal snowflakes fall and melt, and fall and
melt again,
Grant your blessing that I may rest at ease in your
unchanging essence.

Seeing the dawn blaze on the eastern hill, I remember your brilliant smile,
Seeing the deer browse among the pines, I remember your tender way,
Feeling the razor knife of winter wind, I remember
your wrathful power.
Grant your blessing that we may meet in luminous
space beyond conceptions.

Though I can't remember even last night's dream,
Though I couldn't remember then that I was dreaming,
Though I long to dream of you more often than I do,
Grant your blessing that I may never forget you
through all my lives.

Holy guru, grant your blessing that I may celebrate
my human life,
Grant your blessing that I may meet my death
without regret,
Grant your blessing that real compassion for others
may take root in me,
Grant your blessing that I may ride your joyful
naked mind at last.

*This was written at the retreat cabin of Sambhogakaya at the Rocky Mountain Dharma Center on December 30th, 1990, by a fortunate yogin who once chanced to face in the right direction when the supreme crazy wisdom master Chökyi Gyatso appeared in this world to help every sentient being he encountered. May there be a little virtue from this cry of longing. May all beings be joyous and live in safety.*

This solitary retreat is a decisive turning point in my life. Rinpoche's words ten years before—that my time in California is a temporary assignment in a foreign country—return to me with greater clarity than ever. I know now without doubt that it is time to leave, though I still have no clear sense of where I'm headed.

# Chapter 16

My father stands next to me by the shining white structure in which Rinpoche was cremated. It stands as a memorial in a big meadow surrounded by deep green woods, up the hill from the retreat center in Vermont where he first turned the wheel of the dharma in this country. My father is breathing heavily. He will be eighty years old in less than a year, and considering that he has just walked more than half a mile with me up to this place, it is really not surprising that his breath is short. Certainly it is not alarming.

"Pretty good for an old man," I can imagine him saying at that moment.

"Pretty good for an old man," he says, with an expression somewhere between a grimace and a smile.

It will be the last time he will walk with me like this. In only a few months, the long, corrosive illness that will claim his lungs and eventually his life will announce its presence for the first time. It will arrive almost to the day as a kind of grim eightieth birthday gift, one that will remain with him until his last breath.

"So this was the spot," he says.

Around us, the high summer grass of the countryside bends in the gentle wind, like a lush, green ocean that catches the afternoon sunlight and gleams all around us.

"Yes, this was it."

"I remember it quite clearly," he continues. "Your mother and I got up before dawn that day in order to drive up here on time for it."

"Yes. I was impressed. It's four hours from Hartford and you were here before eight."

"And the bagpiper was playing in the mist. And then the mist lifted and the sun appeared."

He looks out over the sea of grass in silence. A tiger swallowtail dips and soars near a clump of yellow flowers only yards from us, then flutters high and away toward the woods.

"And I really appreciated it, too, Dad, that you did. I don't know if I ever told you that."

"No matter. I was glad we came. We wouldn't have wanted to miss it. No thanks were ever necessary."

"But I appreciated it, and still do."

"Especially your mother. She was very moved by the whole thing."

It's that deflection again, in so many of our exchanges with each other, throughout my life. Yet I feel his good heart.

"You took some wonderful photographs, Dad. I still have some of them."

We stand in silence. The clamor of a vast chorus of cicadas suddenly fills the air in all directions. Almost a scream, when you really stop to listen. Probably it has been there the whole time, and I just noticed it, like the background hum of a refrigerator. Two small white cabbage butterflies dance past us.

"How many years is it now?" my father asks.

"It was nine years in May."

He receives this without speaking.

"It seems as if it were only yesterday," I say, aware of the triteness of the remark, but pierced by its truth all the same.

"It seems as if it were only yesterday that I was a boy of seven, chasing butterflies through fields like this," my father says wistfully. His eyes scan the high grass.

"Is that a zebra swallowtail?" he asks, talking more to himself than to me, with that familiar excitement in his voice when he is about to make a delightful little zoological discovery he hadn't expected to make.

"Where?"

"Oh, no. It's just another tiger. My eyes aren't what they used to be. And I'm a little winded. Would it be okay if I sat down?"

"Of course."

He sits on the ledge at the base of the freshly painted white memorial. Just above his head a bright red, artfully painted garland of traditional Tibetan ornamentation shines.

I sit next to him.

"It looks as if they keep this painted fresh and new every year, don't they?" he remarks with a touch of irony.

"It does."

"Seems contrary to Buddhism, somehow."

"How so?"

"With its emphasis on the impermanence of everything, and no ego and all the rest of it. Why not just let it return to earth, naturally?"

"Just a way of honoring who the teacher was, I suppose,"

I respond. I feel the familiar approach of his skeptical mind honing in on the whole subject now, yet I am surprised how little defensiveness I feel.

"That's the thing about religion," he continues.

"What's the thing?"

"Not just religion. Worldly power, too. Needing to enshrine things and make them permanent, make a monument to them. But nothing lasts. 'My name is Ozymandias, king of kings.' Remember that poem?"

"Of course. Shelley. 'Look on my works, ye mighty, and despair!'"

"Right! I probably read that to you fifty years ago. Such a good memory you have."

I laugh, reminding him I've read it a few times since on my own.

"But this feels different than Ozymandias," I add.

"How so?"

"It's not trying to intimidate or impress people that way. Just an acknowledgement of the sacredness, rather than a proclamation of the ego."

"But does sacredness really need that kind of acknowledgement?"

"I don't see that it hurts anyone, that kind of reminder."

"Do you think *he* felt he needed this?"

"Who?"

"Your teacher. Rinpoche."

"I never really thought about it."

"I doubt it. It's the followers who need it. Always. Don't you think? And that's how organized religion just keeps perpetuating itself."

I nod in a noncommittal way without speaking. He doesn't press the point further. We sit in silence. In the summer sky near the horizon above the dark woods a flock of fleecy white clouds drifts by. They are fat, white and puffy, innocent as lambs in a children's story where no one ever dies.

"It seems to me that the real beauty of everything in life is so much tied up in the truth that it doesn't last—whether it's a flower or a piece of music or an entire life."

"So true, Dad."

Above our heads now a red-tailed hawk is circling. My father gazes up at it with a joyful expression.

"Do you remember the rainbows at his cremation?" I ask.

"Yes indeed. And the three eagles circling above us at the end, as well."

"How old was he?" he asks then, still gazing at the hawk.

"Rinpoche?"

"Yes."

"When he died?"

"Yes."

"Forty-seven."

"Damn! So young!"

"Yes."

"Alcohol."

"I suppose."

"Of course it was, Frank. No 'suppose' about it. He was an alcoholic. Surely you're not in denial about that."

He does not turn toward me for a response to his challenge, but looks out over the meadow again, then adds softly:

"I just don't get it."

I am disarmed by his gentleness, feeling how he actually

wants to understand this time, not to prosecute. I realize that I don't really understand, either, and that I never fully will, and that it's okay.

"People asked him again and again, begged him really, to stop," I finally respond.

"And what would he say?"

"'Don't try to interfere with the work I'm doing. I have so much to do and so little time. Just help me.' I'm told that he once said something of that sort."

My father shakes his head without speaking. Together we gaze up at the circling hawk.

"It seems kind of like the lives of great blues artists," my father observes. "Billie Holiday. Charlie Parker. They're brilliant but also self-destructive. They burn so brightly, and burn out so quickly."

"Perhaps. But the Tibetans don't see it that way."

"How do they see it?"

"That he was a great saint, with no regard for himself, interested only in helping others, and willing to do whatever it took."

"But how would being a drunk and shortening your life that way be helpful to others?"

"The Tibetans would say he was a crazy wisdom master who turned poison into medicine."

"What does that mean? I'm a doctor. Poison is poison, and medicine is medicine. And how can wisdom be crazy? It makes no sense."

"In the sense that he didn't care if it was poison for him, as long as his life was medicine for the rest of us. All he cared about was waking people up. He didn't have that sense of self-preservation that most people have."

"It makes no sense, Frank. That part seems just crazy. Period."

"I know it makes no sense to you. He never asked me or anyone else to defend him, so I guess we'll just have to leave it at that."

*With my parents in Crestone, Colorado, 1997. Photograph by Nan Kenney.*

My father shakes his head ruefully: "I knew he died young but I didn't realize he was only forty-seven. It's so sad. How much more he could have done. He was certainly a remarkable fellow. No denying that."

"He did so much, anyway. Amazing when you look at the

whole arc of his life. I never got the sense he regretted not having been able to do more."

"Well, I guess we'll never really know about that point, will we?"

"I guess not."

"Look at that damned hawk, still circling," my father says now, looking up again. "You'd think we were rabbits or something." He looks at his watch.

"Time to get these old bones back down the hill, Frankie boy. Help your old man up."

"Of course." I stand and offer him my arm.

We move, a little stiffly, down the hill. In the sky above us now, the red-tailed hawk drifts lazily away toward the east.

As his breathing becomes more labored and his powerful lifeforce wanes, my father becomes softer and less opinionated in his dealings with other people. He seems mainly sad, very sentimental at times, sitting in his reclining chair and reviewing his life with a bittersweet mixture of satisfaction and regret. Tears come to his eyes easily and often.

His main connection with the present remains what it has always been since I was a child—his flowers. His orchids. Every morning he goes down to his greenhouse by means of the elevator wheelchair my brother has so generously and ingeniously devised for him. Here there is no time for reminiscence or regret. Just an endless creative impulse into which he pours all that remains of his vitality. I see him now in my mind's eye through two archetypal scenes, repeating themselves day after day almost until he can no longer breathe at all.

In one, he sits at his potting bench in the anteroom to his greenhouse, surrounded by red-brick flowerpots, soil and bark, and small orchid seedlings. His hands, large and veined and graceful and still strong, expertly mix the ingredients that will result in new hybrids of orchids, beautiful and exotic and never seen before. As I come down the stairs I can hear the oxygen machine by his side, wheezing, breathing for him. He works with an almost feverish intensity, utterly unaware of my presence.

In the other, he sits in his wheelchair in the middle of his greenhouse, surrounded by hundreds of orchids in bloom, an extravaganza of brilliant yellows, purples, reds, and green foliage everywhere. He exults now in his own church, his own green mansion, wielding the hose with its fine mist of spray, covering each of his treasured creations with the fresh dew of the unceasing beginning of the world, the ever-present morning of life.

His hair, once jet-black and thick, is now pure white, slightly thinning but still luxuriant after eighty-four years. As he works, he listens to the music of Beethoven piped through the speakers at either end of his greenhouse. His shoes and the bottoms of his trousers are drenched with spray. He is happy, forgetful for a few blessed moments of the enemy that is slowly invading his fortress and stealing his life.

Truly his greenhouse is his church, now more than ever, and his flowers are his prayers. He has not set foot inside a church or a temple for at least fifty years. Suspicious of organized religion even to the point of contempt, his favorite parable in this regard is the one where God and the Devil are walking along the road.

"Look, there's the Truth," says God, pointing to a beautiful, gleaming, diamond-like object lying by the side of the road.

"Fantastic, let's organize it," says the Devil.

As his illness progresses, I ask him what he thinks happens when you die, what he thinks will happen to him.

"Probably nothing at all. It just ends, and I return to the earth."

"Are you sure?"

"Of course not. I'm not sure of anything except that my body is giving up on me."

"Suppose that there is something of you—of your mind, I mean—that continues."

"Well, it's not likely, but anything is possible, I suppose."

"Suppose there is."

"Well then, my father's attitude is good enough for me."

"Which was?"

*"I'll take my chances."*

I never completely understand his final word on the subject and, sensing that it is an effort at this point for him to talk this much, don't pursue it further. He turns again fully to watering his orchids. Full sunlight pours through the glass roof, illuminating the beads of spray like tiny, perfect diamonds.

In the final months of his life, my father lives at my sister's home most of the time. She and her husband, both doctors, care for him with great skill and resourcefulness, overseeing his treatment and taking him to the hospital for tests and emergency procedures when necessary. But everyone, most of all he himself, is well aware that all that is now being done for him is palliative. The respiratory tissue of his lungs is steadily turning to useless, calcified pulp, unable to exchange oxygen. The technical term is pulmonary fibrosis. He is using an oxygen tank twenty-four hours a day. He is slowly suffocating to death.

My mother, drawing on her nurse's training of years past, helps him patiently with every ordinary detail as his strength inexorably fails. She walks him to the bathroom and stays with him as he relieves himself. She helps him stand up again. She feeds him. She rubs ointment on the tender skin of his frail back, beneath which the bones now plainly show.

I know the endgame has arrived, though he and I never openly discuss it. Instead, I make every effort to visit him more often, flying the two thousand miles from my home to my sister's home every other weekend for the last five months of his life. Yet even with all the expenditure of time, energy, and money, I don't feel generous enough. I've never felt generous enough with my father.

Or perhaps I've just never felt that the gifts I had to offer him were gifts he really wanted.

I realize in these final months the poignancy of our connection more than ever—that my father has deeply instilled in me from the time I was a child an unquenchable longing for the infinite, but then could never fully support all my adult attempts to explore and actualize that longing. Even though I sense that, in his heart of hearts, he himself has never given up that longing either.

This, I realize, is our real connection—even though we've touched it together less and less often after I've left his home and lived my own life. I wonder what inner resources he is summoning now to meet his death. Yet I am shy to ask.

Hanging out at my sister's home with him, I feel awkward almost to the point of uselessness. Surrounded as he is by family members whose medical knowledge and expertise fully match his own, and who love him and are completely devoted to him, I see that I have no vital role to play in any practical sense. When he needs help and none of the others are there, my attempts to make him comfortable are always well meaning, but clumsy and often counterproductive.

Once, in helping him shift his position in bed, I accidentally disconnect his oxygen. Neither of us notice for a few moments, then he experiences extreme difficulty in breathing and immediately sees the unplugged plastic tube.

"What's happening?" he cries out in panic.

Then in anger toward me, "What the hell are you doing?"

Alternately terrified and furious, he berates me as vehemently as his compromised breathing will allow.

Maintaining my composure as best I can, I apologize to him and calmly reconnect the tube. I notice that my compassion for the intensity of his fear and pain is actually stronger now than my habitual defensiveness at his criticism. He breathes freely again, and relaxes on his bed. His eyes close and he says nothing for several minutes as I sit there. I think he has fallen asleep and I'm about to get up to leave.

"Read to me, will you?" I hear him say.

"I thought you were asleep."

"No, just resting. Just resting."

"What would you like me to read to you?"

"Oh, I don't know." He closes his eyes again. Then he

says brightly, "Wordsworth."

"The one you always used to recite to us?"

"Which one was that?" He closes his eyes and grimaces slightly with the effort of speaking.

"'The World Is Too Much with Us.'"

"Oh, that's a wonderful poem!" He smiles remembering it. "But not that one. The one about immortality."

"Yes. 'Intimations from Early Childhood.' I forget the whole title."

"Yes. That's it. But just that one part."

"I think I know the part you mean. It's a long poem, and a lot of it is corny."

"Yeah, but that one part—

"Our birth is but a sleep and a forgetting—"

"That's it. And it goes on from there … how does it go again?"

"I need to find it. I don't remember it exactly."

"Go see if you can."

I return a few minutes later from my sister's bookcase. The poem is there: "Intimations of Immortality from Recollections of Early Childhood." I find the lines. My father's eyes are closed, but I can feel his attentiveness.

> "Our birth is but a sleep and a forgetting:
> The soul that rises with us, our life's Star,
> Hath had elsewhere its setting,
> And cometh from afar.
> Not in entire forgetfulness,
> And not in utter nakedness,
> But trailing clouds of glory do we come,
> From God, who is our home."

He smiles with that familiar, almost ecstatic expression he can have when he really enjoys something. His eyes are filled with tears.

"Sorry about the way God gets in there," I say.

"It doesn't matter," he says. "That kind of God ..." He gasps for breath. Then he finishes, "I don't object to."

We sit in silence for a while.

"My mind feels the same now as it did when I was a boy," he says then. "Something in me that feels like it's never changed."

He is silent again from the effort of speaking.

"Only my body," he continues. "Christ, Frank, my body."

"Can I rub some ointment on your skin?"

"I look in the mirror and I have no idea who that concentration camp survivor looking back at me is."

Clearly he doesn't want anything from me now except that I listen. Rubbing ointment isn't my job.

"It's so—I can't even think of a word for it."

"Insulting?"

"Oh that, for sure," he says with a rueful little laugh. "But more than that. It's ... it's surreal."

He closes his eyes again. He seems to be struggling with something. Then he opens his eyes and says to me, "Rearrange the family jewels for me, will you, Frank?"

"You mean—"

"Yeah, my balls are stuck under me and it hurts. Just reach in and make them more comfortable."

I do.

"Atta boy. Thanks."

"Atta boy." An expression he hasn't used with me for

forty years at least. We sit in silence again. He closes his eyes, then opens them again and looks directly into mine.

"I can remember the first time I held you at the hospital," he says. "You looked up at me as I looked at you, and I remember thinking, 'He and I know each other. We know each other. We're old friends.'"

"You never told me that story before."

"I never had reason to."

"What's your reason now?"

"No reason. The poem, maybe."

He closes his eyes again.

"I appreciate your telling me now, Dad."

"Sure."

A moment later he grimaces, then commands me in his old way: "Roll me slightly this way if you would. Then find your mother and tell her to come rub my back for me with that lotion of hers."

"Will do."

"And be careful of that oxygen tube this time, damn it."

I help him without further mishap. Then, strangely relieved at this offer of escape from an almost unbearable intimacy, I hastily exit his room and call to my mother.

# Chapter 17

As a little boy, I am athletic, energetic, and mischievous, but also sensitive and very susceptible to teasing. I seem to wear a sign on my back that says Tease Me—which both my younger brothers and the older boys at school are able to read quite clearly. My brothers tease me to equalize our power imbalance in age and strength; the older boys at school tease me because they can and because they take a cruel delight in doing so.

As a second grader, I wear a warm winter coat with a green hood that my mother has picked out for me. For reasons that I cannot understand, the sixth-grade boys stand at the entrance of the school each morning and taunt me with the constant mocking refrain, "Here comes Little Green Riding Hood!"

I ignore it for days as best I can, but finally can stand it no longer and tell my father.

"Don't pay any attention to them," he says calmly. "Just don't let them know it bothers you, and they'll get tired of it and stop."

"I've been trying that, Dad."

"Well, keep doing it."

"I want you to tell them to stop it."

"That wouldn't be a good idea."

"Why not?"

"Because once they know you need me to help you, they'll probably tease you even more once I leave."

"I just want you to tell them to pick on somebody their own size. That's what you always say."

"Maybe you should tell them that, yourself."

"No, I want you to."

"Not yet. Don't give up."

I return to school, and the daily torment continues. Finally, one of the bullies pulls on my hood in the schoolyard, and I lose my balance and fall. Holding back the tears of humiliation, I scramble to my feet and say to him, "Why don't you pick on somebody your own size?"

The oaf lets out a howl of glee. He turns to one of his co-conspirators, shouts at him, "You're my size!" and proceeds to push him around in a transparent pretense of fighting. Both of them turn toward me and laugh uproariously.

Next morning my father drives me to school and waits in his car as I walk into the schoolyard. The same boy comes up and pulls on my hood once more. His friends gather round to enjoy the daily entertainment. Then I see my father get out of the car.

He walks slowly over to the gang of boys. I stand there with renewed hope. I almost want to cheer! I also want to tell them that he's my father, but something makes me think better of it. I remember that he doesn't look angry, and that he doesn't seem to be in a hurry. I've never seen him like this before. At home, when my brothers and I fight past the point of civilized acceptability, he issues a warning or two, then rushes over and spanks us fiercely.

He goes over to the ring of boys and stands directly in front of them.

"What's going on here?" he says in a tone more curious than threatening.

The bully looks down at his feet and says nothing. I want to tell my father that it was him all along, but I keep quiet.

"We were just having a little fun," says another boy in the circle.

My father looks closely at the boy who has just spoken.

"Hmm, fun, eh? It doesn't look like this little guy here is having much fun, do you think?"

Again, he inquires of them in such a matter-of-fact way, as if he were their teacher asking them for the answer to one of their math homework problems. I'm disappointed that he hasn't told them I'm his son. As he stands there, I begin to realize that he isn't going to. I want him to, but I sense he has a reason not to, and that I should keep our secret to myself, even if I'm not good at keeping secrets. Maybe now he's going to tell them to pick on somebody their own size. I wait expectantly.

"Aren't you guys smart enough to find better ways of having fun than hurting a little boy?"

The gang is silent. Heads hang. Feet scuff the dirt.

"I'd think you'd be kind of ashamed of yourselves. After all, it doesn't take much guts to go after someone younger and smaller than you."

His even, reasonable tone is so soothing that you might not even notice how quickly the noose is tightening around this gang of sixth-grade ruffians.

"He's the one who did most of it," says one of the boys,

betraying his comrade. Their alliance has finally begun to show signs of cracking.

"Aren't you a little ashamed, young fella?" my father says gently, almost sorrowfully, to the ringleader who has spearheaded my suffering for the past six weeks. The boy says nothing, but his face reddens. He looks wrathfully over at his classmate—the one who ratted him out.

"If I were you, I think I would be," my father continues. "Especially because I know you don't really want to be a bully. You can do better than that, don't you agree?"

He claps the boy affectionately on the shoulder. The boy looks up quickly, nods his head, and mumbles something that sounds like a halfhearted yes.

"Sure you can," says my father encouragingly, as if he had suddenly become this kid's personal, paternal coach. He squeezes his shoulder now. I feel a twinge of jealousy.

"Now let him go on to his class and find a better way to have fun from now on. Okay?"

The big boys nod as one. I'm struck by how small they look now. Without looking at me or saying good-bye, my father walks back to his car and drives away. They don't tease me again.

But next day I ask my mother to buy me another coat. She says she will discuss it with my father. Soon she comes back to tell me that the coat I have is just fine and I should wear it till I outgrow it, which will probably be in less than a year the way I'm growing.

When I consider my relationship with my father very deeply, I see that it was perfect.

It was perfect despite all of our misunderstandings. It was perfect despite his disappointed hopes and unfulfilled expectations for me. It was perfect despite his need to compete with me. It was perfect despite my vain attempts to live up to his ideas about me, until Rinpoche so kindly showed me that living up to my father's expectations—or anyone's, for that matter—was not the point, and that my life was really about something else altogether.

No, more than that, it was perfect precisely *because* of these things. How else could I ever grow up, without his powerful, magnetic presence and example always in the background of my consciousness? How else could I ever grow up if not by failing, finally, to please him or fulfill his real dreams for me? How else could I slowly and painfully discover who I really was and what I was meant to do in this life without the compelling image of what he seemed to expect of me always pushing against my life?

Despite all his charming denials to the contrary, his expectations of me were like a hard stone, which for so many years I vainly tried to lift and carry, till at last I realized that this stone was there only for me to sharpen my own sword upon. At that point I began to stop struggling, and to enjoy our friendship for what it was. Our friendship was a warrior combat between worthy opponents, connected by a deep, primal affection and loyalty.

He certainly didn't always make it easy. And unlike Rinpoche, the obstacles he put in my path were not the unbiased, accurate reflections of a wakeful and compassionate mirror. No, they were the forceful projections of a flawed and sometimes frightened and insecure man. That I idealized him so much as a boy made those flaws all the more difficult for me to see or accept.

When I was twelve years old, I competed in my school's track-and-field competition. It was a beautiful morning in early June, and I had been excitedly waiting for this Field Day for many months, and even training for it. I was a talented young athlete, and highly competitive as well. I entered the three main events—the fifty-yard dash, the one-hundred-yard dash, and the long jump—and won all three. I was exultant.

My father, who had attended the same school twenty-eight years before, cheered me from the sidelines the entire morning, and proudly watched as the school officials placed three blue ribbons on the breast of my white T-shirt during the closing ceremony. I could see him turn again and again with great happiness and animation toward the fathers of the other boys whom I had defeated. I knew he was telling them that I was his son.

"Atta boy!" he called to me from the crowd.

If a twelve year old is capable of having a peak experience, I had one that morning on that field, with my father there to witness my perfect triumph. Only minutes later, we left the schoolyard together to return home. As we were walking toward my father's automobile, he suddenly turned to me and said, "Let's race the rest of the way to the car. See if you can beat me."

I remember so vividly, so indelibly, how much my heart sank in that moment. We had often had footraces with each other since my early boyhood. He had been a very fast runner himself as a young man and wanted me to push myself to keep up with him. Perhaps two years before, the trajectories of my increasing speed and his declining speed had finally crossed. I beat him by a hair. He acknowledged it graciously, even with a certain pleasure.

"That's it, Frankie. You've outrun your old man. I'm retiring from our competition." Though I didn't know then what a rite of passage was, he had certainly just bestowed one on me.

Why did he have to challenge me now? I realized that the reasons didn't matter. Whatever they might have been, he would blithely have denied them if confronted with them. All that mattered was the fact of it. In that moment, he took all my blue ribbons away, even though I would display them on my bedroom shelf till I left home for good and went to college.

We raced those fifty yards to the car, *and I let him win.*

For whatever reason, I felt that I had no other choice. We drove home in silence. And I remember wondering as we drove—who's the father now, and who's the son?

# Chapter 18

Waking up at dawn one morning while on vacation in Mexico, I know instantly that this is the day of my father's death. I dress quickly, hurry to the rental car, and head for the Internet café and the nearest telephone, eight miles away. The sun is just rising. My wife Nan is still asleep.

We are staying in a thatched palapa on a beautiful, remote beach in Tulum on the Yucatán Peninsula. We made plans to come here more than six months ago, and are halfway through the ten-day vacation. We have had no electronic contact with anyone since we got here. Each morning up until this one, we have begun the day swimming in a placid, lime-green ocean warm as a baby's bath—the first time since my childhood that I haven't been even slightly fearful of the water. Ironic to consider, in retrospect, how that fear began when I was six years old, and dived into Blue Mountain Lake in the Adirondacks without knowing how to swim. My father, a few steps behind me on the pier down which I ran and off which I dived, fished me out of the deep cold water and saved my life.

I am enjoying the sweetest holiday of my life.

I asked my father's permission two weeks before, having spent every other weekend of the past five months with him.

I know there's a real chance he might die while we're gone.

On one hand, by canceling our plans, we demonstrate our loyalty and love to him; and by following through with them, our selfishness. Yet on the other, by canceling our plans we give him the message that we're expecting him to die anytime, and just hanging around waiting for it to happen; while by going forward with our own lives, we express a vote of confidence in his own tenacious ability to go on living. It's a double bind.

"What do you think, Dad? We can certainly postpone this if you want us to."

"Of course not," he replies without hesitation. "You've worked very hard these past few months. Enjoy yourself!"

"How are you feeling?"

"Great! I feel like a racehorse about to leave the starting gate," he enthuses over the wheezing of his oxygen tank.

The next day he's going to return to his own home for the first time in months, leaving the seamless, well-oiled cocoon of care he's received from my sister and my brother-in-law since the beginning of the year. We all know the risks. He knows them, most of all.

"Have a great time! When you come back and I see you again, I'll stand up and offer you my chair!"

What a strange thing to say! I think to myself, even at the time. It's the last time I see him alive, and the last thing he says to me face to face …

"You should probably come home right away if you want to see your father again."

My mother's voice, sad but firm, crackles through the wires of the phone in the shabby Mexican village.

"Can I speak to him?"

A gap. Then I hear his voice, very feeble on the line.

"Dad, we're coming home right now to see you."

"Oh, won—" He has hardly enough breath to utter more than one syllable at a time.

"Wonder—" he finally murmurs.

"Don't tire yourself out talking to me now. I'll see you later today."

"Okay."

"I love you, Dad."

"I love … you … Frank."

"Good-bye, Dad."

I hear a series of fumbling clicks and the line goes dead.

An hour later, we're stopped by the police for speeding on the way to the airport to make the next flight back to the States. My Spanish is primitive and my emotions are high.

"Mi padre. Muerte! Por favor. Mi padre."

They toy with us for several precious minutes while I desperately repeat "Mi padre muerte" like a mantra, hoping perhaps for some kind of sacred magic to shift this impasse. Finally I slip them two twenties, afraid they'll just keep it and demand more. But they let us go on our way.

Twelve hours and three flights later, we land at the airport five miles from my parents' home. It is a balmy spring night in Connecticut. A light steady rain has begun to fall. My brother is waiting for us at the boarding gate. One look at his face and I know before a word is spoken.

My father is dead.

He is lying in his own bed next to his open bedroom window. My mother lies on her bed next to his, head in her pillow, sobbing quietly with a gentle yet primal sound that mingles grief, exhaustion, and relief. His breathing stopped half an hour before we arrived, but his lifeforce remains palpable, almost electric, in the room where he lies.

I sit with his body through the night, in a chair right next to his bed. Berating myself fiercely, *Why couldn't I get here on time?* then letting it go. *My brother and sister were here to help him at the end! Where was I?* Letting it go. Letting it go. *I'm so sorry, Dad.* Letting it go. Just sit.

I have never felt so awake. I could sit with him like this for days if asked to do so.

I watch the features of his face change, soften and relax. As the night goes on, the lines of age and illness and care seem to recede. How handsome, even noble he looks—as he did when I was a boy and treasured his every utterance and his every gesture. His mouth with its strength and sensuality. His long, luxuriant wisps of untamed white hair, like soft uncut grass upon the rock of his skull. Delicately they frame the perfect chiseled bones of his nose, his jaw, his cheeks, his forehead.

This is the final illusory flowering of his male perfection. This is his final gift to me.

Every half hour I touch his hand or his face. Gradually, inexorably, they grow colder. The subtle force of his presence begins to fade a little. More now like a sculpture than a human being as he lies there. The night flows on. My thoughts flow on with it, a deep river of recollection—sadness, joy, gratitude, humor, regret, relief.

Thinking. Come back to this room. Come back to this moment.

Just before dawn the birds start. It sounds as if all the

birds in the world are out there just beyond my father's window this morning. The rain has not stopped. It continues, gentle and steady, and will not stop for three days, not until the morning after his funeral. By a striking coincidence, my father is buried on the 26th of May, the same day as Rinpoche's cremation, fourteen years before.

My mother comes in first. She has slept in an upstairs room. She tells me: "There's a Baltimore oriole at the feeder right now! Your father and I saw it once last spring and never again after that. We kept looking for it. It's back!"

"That's wonderful, Mom!"

"It's back, Frank. I feel that it's your father, or that he's sent it. I feel it so strongly."

"I'm sure you're right, Mom." I stand and give her a long, tender hug.

An hour later, Uncle Bill arrives. He's driven up from New York. He enters my father's room and sits on the bed next to him. His eyes fill with tears. "Your father," he says to me, "Your father was a great man. He was the best man I ever knew. He was the man I always wanted to be."

My nephews arrive next, with their springer spaniel puppy in tow. She bounds into the bedroom, leaps up onto my father's bed and runs wildly over his body. First there is panic, then a few disapproving shouts of "No!" and "Bad dog!" Then everyone bursts out in laughter.

That night I leaf through my father's tattered Shakespeare—the one from which he read to us when we were boys. Looking for appropriate lines to read at his funeral, I notice a small yellow Post-it paper protruding from the massive volume, and open to the page it marks.

It is the final act of *Hamlet*. My father has marked in pencil Hamlet's parting words to his dearest friend Horatio, just before he goes to meet his death in the duel with Laertes:

> There is special providence in the fall of a sparrow. If it be now, 'tis not to come; if it be not to come, it will be now; if it be not now, yet it will come: the readiness is all—since no man has aught of what he leaves, what is it to leave betimes?

Let be.

# Epilogue

Rinpoche has been gone from this world many years longer than the entire span of time he spent here in America, teaching the dharma and fully embodying its profound truth in every interaction with every person he ever met. Yet I am unable to think of him, ever, in the past tense. In my heart, this passage of time—both while he was alive and since his death—is an illusion.

But when I look in the mirror and see the dark brown hair of my youth turned to gray, the lines of my face deepened, the muscles of my body more slack, that passage of time is also real and undeniable. Having seen both my teacher and my father die, I can no longer harbor any illusions that my own death is not drawing steadily nearer on the horizon ahead of me.

> The world and its inhabitants are impermanent,
> Especially the life of beings is like a bubble;
> Death is real and comes without warning,
> This body will be a corpse.

(from "The Four Thoughts That Turn the Mind Toward the Dharma," a Tibetan text)

As time has passed, Rinpoche's presence has become more and more vivid and penetrating for me. Freed from the reference points of his crippled body and even from the little landmarks of memory of the specific experiences I had of him—the experiences I retell in this book—the inexhaustible energy of his being haunts me on a daily basis. Indeed, if I rely only on my memories of him, I get caught in the trap of nostalgia—a net in which I can never find him, no matter how hard or how cleverly I may try.

"The only nostalgia a warrior should have," he once said, "is nostalgia for the present moment."

And so, more and more, he has become the secret, transparent body of my personal world. At times his message is gentle and soothing, at times abrupt, terrifying, electric. His face smiles, or leers, within all the little ups and downs of my daily life.

There is no escape. And I do not want there ever to be any escape.

At the same time, my life moves forward a few years after his death with a sudden ease and a freedom from obstacles—out of California, out of my unhappy marriage, and into a new phase of my life as a psychotherapist, trained at Naropa, and a university professor there, teaching the dharma to the next generation of spiritual seekers.

In a very ordinary sense, I experience the satisfaction of a fruition I haven't known before. There is no longer the old conflict between who I am and how I make a living. Every day, I am what I do. I cherish my students and my clients, and feel each day that my work with them is a sacred calling. Especially in the case of my students, I am amazed at how much wiser they are than I was at their age. As Rinpoche told us, "The children will surpass their parents." I am even more amazed that they feel I have something to teach them.

Most joyfully, I meet the woman who will become my third wife. Nan's beauty and dazzling smile are the first things, of course, to arrest my attention. But beyond that, her depth keeps revealing itself further as we spend more and more time together. She is kind, she is wise, she is earthy and grounded from her life experiences—two children by the age of twenty-one, her first grandchild by thirty-nine. She is tough-minded and direct, but never judgmental. Not since my encounters with Rinpoche years earlier, have I met a friend who could be counted upon to tell me the truth with such fearless honesty. Nor have I met another one since!

*Nan in Bhutan, 2005. Photograph by the author.*

The day the divorce decree for my second marriage finally comes through, and the financial settlement with it, I complain bitterly to Nan about how unfair I think it is.

As if in an echo of Rinpoche's command to me ten years earlier, even though she never met him, she says:

"You have to accept this and stop complaining about it. Every time you complain, you bring that negative energy into our relationship. It's not good. It has to stop."

"I know. I just don't seem to be able to get past it."

"You never had children. You never had to carry that burden and responsibility. Maybe if you practice seeing her as the child you never had, it will be easier for you to take on this weight without being so resentful about it."

"I feel she's trying to rip me off."

"She's obviously just scared. She's not a bad person. You're the man and you're in the power position."

And I do eventually go forward without any resentment toward Helen. Three years later, Nan and I marry. With each year, my happiness grows. I enjoy my life, fully and deeply.

Now, when I am asked to teach something about Rinpoche outside the framework of all the dharma and Shambhala Training seminars I have taught over nearly thirty years, the title *No Hope, No Fear: Quintessential Chögyam Trungpa* flashes immediately in my mind.

"No hope" because his constant message to us is that it is impossible for our ego to attain enlightenment. It is, as he said once, like trying to attend your own funeral.

It is not that life itself is hopeless—far from it! That is the fixated mistake of the nihilist—a view that leads to depression and despair. There is nothing despairing about the warrior's hopelessness.

On the contrary, giving up hope is a path full of clarity, energy, and humor. We can stop trying so earnestly to attain the goal of being Buddha. We can stop postponing the realization that we already are a Buddha. As the Zen saying goes, we should kill the Buddha if we meet him on the road. We can give up the tedious illusion of control, and the poverty mentality that our freedom is always in the future. There is no hope? Fantastic! The life we ordered has already arrived! We will live it! Then no hope becomes no regret.

"No fear" because his constant message to us is that fear itself is not the obstacle. The refusal to acknowledge its pervasive presence in our lives is the obstacle. We must cop to the fear, acknowledge the fear, and relax with the fear. We must see that all the unnecessary suffering and difficulty we create for ourselves and others invariably begins with trying to pretend that the fear isn't there.

As we grow older, the fear doesn't disappear; its object merely keeps changing. Instead of worrying about grades, we worry about money. Instead of freaking out about pimples, we freak out about wrinkles. If meditation practice has any value at all, I hear him saying, it is in helping us see all this with a sense of humor and kindness, and then going forward with our lives with the attitude that fear is our ally and our friend.

Then there is truly no fear, because it has become the rich compost for our warrior garden. It has nourished the flowers of joy, compassion, and courage in our daily lives.

And "quintessential Chögyam Trungpa" because everything he taught us keeps coming back somehow to no hope and no fear.

This is merely my own particular idiosyncratic lens for taking in the unconditioned vastness of who he is and what he has left behind in this world. Once again, I am a blind man touching the elephant. As if I could pour his whole ocean into my little cup! Hopeless!

The first time I try to teach what I learned from Rinpoche in this manner, I get sick on the opening night of the weekend seminar. I feel weak and feeble. This has never happened to me before in my years as a teacher. I can feel that there is a very different energy happening than usual, but try stubbornly to push through the obstacle. I take medicines and supplements. I give even more talks, and longer talks, than I had intended to.

Remembering Rinpoche's fearless willingness to dissolve any sense of boundary between himself and his own students, I throw myself into the weekend without reservation or caution. I meet individually with every student.

In telling these newer students the story of what I imagine was most significant about his life, and especially about his coming to America, I find myself dwelling on his auto accident in Scotland the year before he moved to the United States.

The accident, which left him physically crippled for the remainder of his life, marked a profound turning point. He gave up his monastic robes, married, and let himself come out completely from behind the mystique of ancient Tibetan spirituality in order to teach the dharma in a completely authentic and unprecedented way to the "modern" world of the West.

As the weekend goes on, I begin to feel stronger. I have a palpable sense that I am riding on Rinpoche's blessings, even channeling his lifeforce. The intense interest of a new generation of students in his vivid life and potent teachings gives me tremendous energy. Even the weather shifts—from snow and bitter cold the first evening to unseasonably mild, brilliant sunshine the final day.

By the end of the seminar I am intoxicated with an almost giddy energy and confidence. In addition to my honorarium, the students give me a generous teacher's gift of cash and four beautiful fired-clay cups for tea or sake or whatever I might desire. They toast my teaching efforts with heartfelt enthusiasm. It all goes to my head like champagne bubbles, though I do not really see this clearly yet.

A colleague asks me if I would like him to drive me home, given how ill I was feeling barely more than twenty-four hours ago. One of the students, he informs me, would be happy to drive my car in caravan behind us. All I have to do is sit back and relax and allow others to help me. Exuberant and laden with gifts and the heady memory of so much praise for my work, I decline.

I start the eighty-five mile drive home. Though it is the middle of February, the weather is now warm enough for a convertible, and I wish I could put the top of the roof of my own car down to feel the wind in my face, the way I did when I was nineteen and borrowed my father's car. But I can't. Instead, I simply drive faster, passing every car on the road.

Every so often I look over at all my loot—the wad of bills pushing out of an envelope and the beautiful cups—lying next to me in the passenger seat. I'm almost inebriated with a strange new sense of power. It is primitive, young—like the little boy with his fantasies of tigers and trucks.

Halfway home, I suddenly feel the energy draining out of my body, as if someone had just pulled out the stopper in a full bathtub. At the time, I am speeding at nearly eighty miles an hour. A few hundred yards ahead is the exit from the main highway onto an old back road we always used before the highway was built.

Incredibly, I have the presence of mind to get off the main road right away and slow down. Immediately after the exit, I see a little gravel road leading to a weedy, abandoned old parking area near some woods. A fleeting thought arises that I should pull off there, *right now*, rest for a few minutes, and call Nan to tell her where I am and what's happening. There's a café half a mile up the road, and after a short rest I will drive there, get some coffee, then drive the rest of the way home.

But I brush that thought aside with another one: I will drive to the café first, *then* rest and call my wife from there. I keep driving, thirty-five miles an hour now, on a two-lane road. I will be at the café in just a minute or two—no more than that …

I am awakened by the sound of gravel beneath the wheels of my car, and by the sensation of the passenger side tilting precipitously downward. As if in a dream I watch myself in a hurtling metal box in a culvert crammed with snow-covered scrub and saplings. The rigid box bounces mercilessly along through the ditch, and my tender body bounces up and down with it.

I flash back and forth between watching all this from a slight distance, like the director of a film, and being utterly embedded in it, like the doomed character in the film. I feel the uneasy conversation of metal with bone begin.

Oh, of course! I realize at last. My car is about to crash! There's no time for fear, but what I do feel is no doubt born from profound fear: A strange *irritation*! A sense of disbelief, coupled with a thought that arises in my still slightly dreamy mind with pristine clarity:

*This isn't how my life is supposed to end!*

Oh, the unendurable pain now of my pride, my absurd delusion of specialness. Every few minutes someone in the world dies just like this. I am *not* special.

My car threads an improbable needle's eye between the concrete abutment of a small bridge and a tree much larger and more immovable than any of the bracken my car has been plowing through.

The thought flashes—a thought very like the kinds of thoughts I had that spring night on LSD in New Haven, nearly forty years ago:

*There is no "supposed to." No one else is writing this script. I am alone.*

Fully, helplessly awake now. My car rattles over the little icy streambed that the bridge spans, up a short slope toward a stand of small trees. I'm aware of the brilliant afternoon light slanting like diamond needles down through those bare trees, off the glistening snow, through my windshield, and into the car. It is a beautiful, mild false-spring moment in a February woods in Colorado.

Like lightning the thoughts flash:

> *How beautiful! Life goes on without me ...*
> *Life goes on without me. Without me ... Really ...*
> *What have I been thinking all my life?*

The small trees march toward me. I have no relationship with the brakes of my car, and have not since I first realized I'd left the road. For the first time, I relax, a hint of surrender, of not caring.

*This will be over very soon. And I will either be alive at that moment, or not.*

Then everything stops for an instant. Sunlight pours in through the windshield and into my eyes. Blinded by the light, just as on my trip which ended forty years ago.

*Am I dead?*

Then a knifelike sensation of pain as my chest hits the steering wheel of my car.

*Pain! I must still be alive!*

The realization that I'm still alive, I see in retrospect, was the signal to start struggling again. I gasp for breath. The pain is claustrophobic but reassuring. My eyes take in the floor in front of the passenger seat, where the money and cups are now strewn. I feel if I stay in this box I will die. I must get out.

I turn and push open the door. The pain in my chest returns with even greater intensity. I try to rise out of my seat. Something binds me. My seatbelt. Had I not been wearing it, it would not have been my chest and the steering wheel that met so pitilessly, but my head and the windshield.

Then, like a band of angels, men from the trailer park across the road come streaming down the embankment toward my car. Outside on their front porches on this unseasonably warm Sunday afternoon, they saw my car go off the road. Within moments, they pull me out, carry me to safety, call 911, and secure my belongings. Soon the ambulance arrives to take me to the hospital, and a tow truck hauls away my totaled car.

I've suffered a clean fracture of the sternum, but no other internal injuries. I undergo seven weeks of healing, buoyed by the love and concern of my wife and so many friends. The universe has been merciful this time. When I return to the trailer park to pick up my things, certain that the money will be gone, every dollar is in the envelope. And the four cups are still there. At first they look to be completely unscathed. Then I notice that one has a small chip at its rim.

I think of Rinpoche's many warnings to his students about the consequences of not paying attention to the messages from the phenomenal world. It is the principle of the *mahakala*, the great wrathful protector that guided him through the Himalayas and out of Tibet, just ahead of the pursuing Chinese army. The protector is not a separate deity up there, or out there; it is the protecting power of our own awareness and heedfulness. When we are humbly and mindfully in tune with things as they are, the protector does not need to give us messages. When we are not, its feedback can be heavy-handed and even devastating.

This time, in response to all my carelessness and pride, it has given me a penetrating message. It has also spared my life. It has been wrathful and merciful to me at the same time.

I return to that back road in May and retrace the path of my accident. I see that I drove nearly a quarter of a mile on a straightaway without even any glimmer of consciousness, and somehow without meeting any car coming down that two-lane road in the opposite direction. Then, where the road curved gently to the left and crossed the bridge, my car kept going straight, down into the culvert, over the river, and through the woods.

That bare, snowy landscape of three months ago is now lush and green, and the icy February streambed is now in full flow. I search the ground at the base of the clump of trees I'm sure were the ones I hit that afternoon, and find several fragments of plastic from the broken headlight of the car. On one of the trees directly above the fragments is a raw gash that is already beginning to heal.

Standing there in the warm spring sunshine in the little grove across from the trailer park, I reflect upon the truth of my ordinariness, my vulnerability, and my good fortune. I give thanks to the protectors for sparing my life, and gently tie a traditional white silk offering scarf around the wounded trunk of that sturdy young tree.

Alone there in the little grove, I realize that it has taken me a very long time to grow up, and that there is still much more for me to learn. Touching my hand to the bark of the wounded, hardy sapling, I reflect once more upon the truth that neither my teacher—nor my father—ever gave up on me, and my eyes fill with tears of gratitude.

*Thank you … Thank you … Thank you!*

Frank W. Berliner

## Morning Song for My Father

Dawn.
Blue heron stands so still in the silence.
Do you see him now?
                    Look!
Standing
        so still in silence
                    so still
                            in the dawn.
Look at cardinal's crest
                shimmering still in scarlet sun.

Listen to warbler unseen singing from secret woods
      in green sunlight
                in golden shadow singing still
                      in the child's secret heart.
Emptying her gladness now into clear deep sky—
Do you hear her now?
                Listen!
And look at each tree still tender with new leaves!

*In the child's secret heart all gleams there still.*

## Song of Remembrance in Sadness and Joy

*For Chögyam Trungpa Rinpoche*

Gone longer now than ever you were here with us,
Miraculous comet blazing in our dark sky.

I still here, still scared to die, still knowing
My smallness in the vast space of your reality,
Knowing the futility of all my selfish schemes,
But stubbornly persisting out of dead habit,
Sad unendingly for myself and all that lives to die,
Both what I love and what I don't love alike.

Grateful to you always for your overwhelming genuineness,
For telling me the truth fearlessly in every encounter,
For your magical display and tender accuracy,
For your fathomless eyes and ironic smile,
For your never giving up on me,
For this endless, bittersweet, unrequited love affair.

All that you taught was perfect.
In its clear light I recall myself with embarrassment and forgiveness.
Slowly this hard, proud heart of mine cracks,
Like a rock freezing and thawing again and again
Helplessly letting the small, sweet flower of your love
Grow up from it at last.

Good morning, sir!
How may I serve you today?

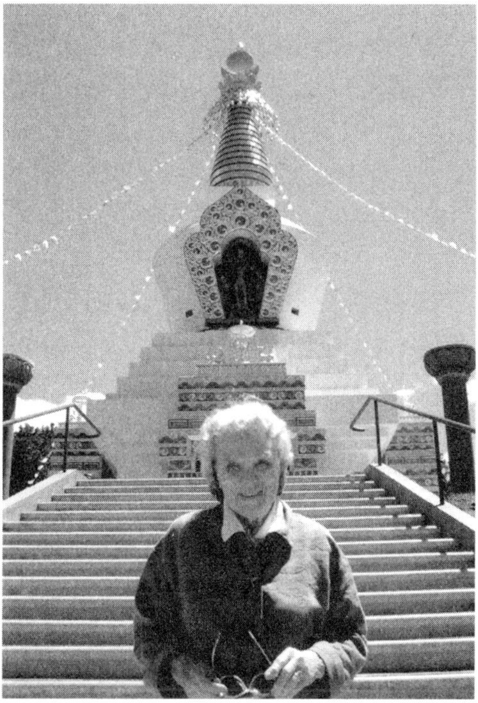

*My mother at the Great Stupa of Dharmakaya, a monument built to honor Chögyam Trungpa Rinpoche's life and work, 2007. Photograph by the author.*

# Acknowledgements

Publishing this book has been a team effort—an effort without which it could never have appeared in print.

I wish to thank Erich Strom for his skillful copyediting; Sandy Lardinois for her careful proofreading; Gail Nelson for her patient and elegant work in designing the book; Alex Musat for his inspired labor in designing and executing the beautiful cover; and Jerry Gentry for his steady hand in guiding the book through the final printing stage.

Most of all I wish to thank Jennifer Holder, who both oversaw and assisted in every aspect and stage of the process. Tirelessly and with unwavering confidence, she midwifed the birth of this memoir from beginning to end. I am profoundly grateful to her.